The Essential Book of Interviewing

THE ESSENTIAL BOOK OF INTERVIEWING

EVERYTHING YOU NEED TO KNOW

FROM BOTH SIDES OF THE TABLE

ARNOLD B. KANTER

TIMES **T** BOOKS

RANDOM HOUSE

Library of Congress Cataloging-in-Publication Data

Kanter, Arnold B.
   The complete book of interviewing : everything you
need to know from both sides of the table / Arnold B.
Kanter.
       p.   cm.
   Includes bibliographical references and index.
   ISBN 0-8129-2281-6
   1. Employment interviewing.   I. Title
HF5549.5.I6K358   1995
650.14—dc20   94-27672

Manufactured in the United States of America
9 8 7 6 5 4 3

To all the interviewees who sat in a
room alone with a guy they didn't know,
taught him about interviewing, and left
him with this bookful of memories, to boot

Acknowledgments

Special thanks to Joanna Klink for her thorough research, perceptive comments and constant encouragement.

My friend and college classmate Peter Osnos, at Random House, said, "Let's do this book," and made it happen. Janie Winkler prepared the manuscript, over and over again. My editor, Henry Ferris, shaped the structure of this book, tightened its prose and made me miss several Cubs games revising the book. Carol Kanter and Jodi Kanter read the manuscript and provided valuable suggestions. Susan Benton-Powers provided helpful input for the chapter on "Achieving Diversity and Avoiding Discriminatory Questions" and the Appendix. Jim Burruss taught me the importance of the climate and managerial style material in "Preparing for the Interview: Interviewer."

Contents

Introduction

Unlike, say, open-heart surgery, everybody thinks he's an expert in interviewing. After all, it's just talking to someone, isn't it? And we've all done that. So what's the big deal?

But being able to talk to someone doesn't make you an accomplished interviewer any more than being able to jog a bit makes you a champion sprinter, or being able to slop a little paint on a canvas makes you Picasso. Indeed, you might wonder why we would even be tempted to assume our interview expertise, when we would not assume our athletic or artistic prowess.

Assumed expertise has serious consequences for both interviewer and interviewee. If you think you know all you need to know about interviewing, you won't take time to reflect on what you are doing to improve your performance. Why should you? You don't study how to carry on a conversation with a friend, do you?

Assumed expertise perpetuates interviewing mistakes. When training a company's interviewers, I often hear, "We'd like you to concentrate on our newer interviewers because they need it most. Our more senior people are pretty good at it. After all, they've been doing it for years."

I am reminded of the story a friend of mine, Dave, tells about the time he was driving down a two-lane road in southern Illinois, doing about sixty miles an hour. He noticed a tractor riding quite a distance ahead of him on the right shoulder of the road. Just before Dave reached the tractor, the farmer driving it crossed in front of him, without warning, pulling onto a dirt path on the left side of the road. Dave slammed on the brakes and screeched to a halt, narrowly avoiding a collision. Furious, my friend pulled off the highway, got out of his car and began shouting at the farmer, "What the hell were you doing, crossing the road like that without looking and without giving any signal? You almost got us killed." The farmer shook his head in disbelief and replied, "Why, you crazy son of a gun, I've been makin' that same darn turn onto this here road every day for twenty-seven years."

The business world, I'm afraid, is loaded with veteran interviewers who have been "conductin' that same darn interview," though most of them, happily, not for twenty-seven years. My experience conducting interviewer-training programs confirms this. Repeatedly I see senior officers make basic mistakes. Not only does that affect their own performance, but it rubs off on others within the company who observe them, as well. Worse still, it affects future generations who, when they become interviewers, repeat the questions they were asked thinking, "This must be the way the game is played."

On the other side of the table, I see interviewees giving the same safe, conventional answers to the conventional questions they are asked. They fancy themselves experts at figuring out what interviewers want to hear. And, by golly, they give it to them.

Let me give both sides permission to break this insidious cycle. You don't have to ask the same questions you were asked (and hated) as an interviewee by those "expert" interviewers who probably asked those questions because they were asked the same questions when they were interviewees. And you don't have to provide the same conventional answers, either.

Our Approach

Throughout this book, we will look at interviewing from both sides of the table. That's because, unlike a lecture or an interrogation, an interview is an *exchange* of information. So, although one party may be called "interviewer" and the other "interviewee," both parties play both roles. When a candidate asks questions about the job, he is acting as interviewer. Similarly, when the employer answers a candidate's questions, she acts as interviewee. So reading only those portions of the book directed at your current position will give you just half the picture you need.

There's another reason to read all of this book. You can do an effective job of interviewing from *either* side of the table only if you understand, and incorporate into your own interview approach, the perspective of the person on the other side. Therefore, throughout the book I've sprinkled notes to the interviewee in sections aimed primarily at the interviewer, and vice versa.

Interviewers and interviewees may also want to look at books in the market directed at advising those who sit on the opposite side of the table from you. Besides giving you a sense of how the other party may be approaching the process, you will see how much we interviewing "experts" disagree.

Many of these books contain diagrams, arrows, and

charts, as well as hokey suggestions such as determining what you are looking for in a job by pretending you are a six-year-old responding to a genie who has just emerged from a lamp to grant you three wishes. Diagrams and genies may have value for others. For me, though, they are not useful; you will not find them in this book.

Nor will this book teach you how to outsmart the other person at the table through conniving tricks. There are plenty of books that teach you how to do that. Beware, though; a lot of those books contain bad advice.

I have read books that advise you intentionally to misinterpret a question you do not wish to face in order to avoid answering it. Others suggest that you subtly use sex to your advantage in the interview, or that you dress in red and give away Valentine candies on February 14. As one of my daughters would say, "Puh-lease, give me a break."

There may indeed be tricks that work in an interview, and the line between a trick and a legitimate interview technique may sometimes seem fuzzy. But I believe firmly that there are limits as to how far an interviewer or interviewee should be willing to go in order to hire somebody/get a job. Those who would go beyond those limits are not the type of employer I would work for, the kind of employee I would hire, or the reader I would want to write for.

The Game

Imagine an ideal world. There's this job. There's this employer who needs to fill this job. There's this interviewee who wants a job. They meet. They talk. They tell each other everything—the employer about the company and the job; the interviewee about him or herself—truthfully. Together, they determine whether this interviewee and this job are a good match. The answer is yes (or no). And (in either case) they all live happily ever after.

Why does this seem like such a fairy tale? Because few people view the job interview as a joint effort to find a good match or to determine that a match does not exist. Instead, both sides view it as a game.

For the employer, the object of the game becomes to sell the job and her company while hiding any blemishes either may possess. At the same time, she tries to ferret out "the truth" about the interviewee, assuming he is trying to hide that truth.

The interviewee's goal in the game is to receive an offer. To accomplish that objective, he presents himself in a way designed to appeal to what he thinks the interviewer wants, whether or not that picture reflects his true self.

Of course, it's not hard to see that the end result of this gamesmanship will be poor job selection from both sides of the table. But if playing an interview game leads to poor job choices, why do so many people play?

The ideal situation in which the interviewer and interviewee tell each other the whole truth assumes there are plenty of jobs to go around. In a tight job market, that may not be true. Or even if it were true, interviewees may not be prepared to act as if it were. And that, of course, affects the interview process. Square interviewees try to squeeze themselves into round jobs.

Likewise, employers become much pickier, sometimes seeking people who are overqualified for the positions. Hiring overqualified people is often a bigger mistake than hiring somebody underqualified. The latter may grow into her job, but overqualified people become unhappy employees who infect others' morale and then leave. Conversely, in a seller's market employers scurry to hire candidates, accepting people who do not meet their criteria.

Another reason participants play an interview game is because they take a short-term view of life. If you desperately need a job to support your family, you may not pay much attention to whether the job is right for your interests and abilities. The stronger the need—or more accurately, the stronger the *perception* of the need—the more your job choice and interview behavior may be distorted.

Likewise, an employer may feel a short-term need to fill a position quickly. A severe shortage of staff may convince you to lower your standards, just to get somebody (some body) on board. And the stronger the perceived need, the more you may deviate from your normal standards, or describe the job or the company in overly glowing terms.

The final reason people play the interview game is inherent in our definition of the ideal situation, which assumes there is *one* right job for every interviewee and *one* right candidate for every position. Though hardly anyone would admit to holding such a belief, many interviewers and interviewees behave as if it were true. That raises the level of anxiety on both sides, distorts the interview process, and encourages the participants to engage in gamesmanship in order to accomplish their objectives.

Now that we understand why so many people play, let's explore how to get beyond the interview game.

The Essential Book of Interviewing

ONE

PREPARING FOR THE INTERVIEW: Interviewer

The most serious interview mistakes both interviewers and interviewees make are made *before* the interview. For both, they involve failure to confront adequately the question, "What am I looking for?" If you haven't confronted that question *before* the interview, even the most effective interview techniques will not compensate for that failure. As that famous philosopher Yogi Berra once put it, "If you don't know where you are going, you will wind up somewhere else."

Not knowing what you are looking for amounts to playing an interview game without even understanding the object of that game. This seems so simple, to consider what you are looking for. Why then is it so often overlooked?

Generally it's not overlooked—entirely. The key word is *adequately* confronting the question. Most interviewers and interviewees would say they know what they are looking for. After all, most companies have an interviewee-evaluation form they can point to that lists characteristics they want in candidates. Similarly, most interviewees have given at least cursory thought to the sort of things they might expect of their job and their employer. But few employers or interviewees have invested the significant amount of time it takes to give systematic thought to the question "What am I looking for?"

How should you approach this analysis? Let's take the company first. To do the analysis effectively, you've got to approach it from several different perspectives.

Supervisor's View

Most employers address the question of what they are looking for by asking those who will supervise the person(s) being hired what characteristics they think they ought to look for in candidates. Chances are they come up with a reasonable-looking list. Let's suppose you try that exercise and come up with this list:

> intelligent
> personable
> motivated
> diligent
> team player
> good writer
> discreet

Sounds like a respectable list. Great, so that's done, now we can go out and interview.

Unfortunately, that's the level of sophistication many companies reach in identifying what they are looking for in candidates. (Indeed, some do not reach even this level of sophistication. They define the job solely in terms of technical skills, ignoring entirely the interpersonal skills necessary for success.) What's wrong with the approach of asking supervisors for a list of characteristics? At least the following:

- It may be the wrong list (supervisors often list characteristics they would ideally like to possess themselves, rather than what is required for the job).
- It may be an incomplete list.
- It does not define the characteristics in a way that would allow an interviewer to know whether the person he is talking to possesses the characteristics.
- It does not define what the job requires somebody to do.
- It does not take the culture of the company into account.
- It does not distinguish the relative importance of the various characteristics.

So how can we avoid these pitfalls? Perhaps, instead of starting by asking supervisors to list the characteristics they are looking for, we should ask them to define what the job requires. This is a way of checking whether the characteristics they believe are necessary to perform the job are in fact necessary. Ask them to answer the question "What does a person have to DO in this job?" When we ask that question, we may come up with a list something like the following:

- Work with people in the (specific list of) departments.
- Identify several action choices for the company.
- Recommend one choice to management.
- Write a report containing that recommendation and explain the basis for it.
- Produce reports within a short time period.
- Present reports orally to management and defend your conclusions.

- Relate to clients with respect to your area of responsibility.

Once we have identified the actual tasks a person must perform in the position, it becomes easier to assess the specific characteristics a candidate must have in order to perform those tasks. Thus, for example, in order to work with people from other departments, an employee may need the following skills:

> good listener
> respects others
> able to understand what other departments do
> able to convince others to help him
> empathy for others' concerns

The above are only hypotheses as to what characteristics the task may require. In a particular situation, some of these may not apply. And, of course, there may be other hypotheses as to what characteristics it takes, as well. Once you have identified these hypotheses, test them out with the supervisors who have identified the tasks. You can make a similar analysis of what characteristics each of the tasks in whatever list you develop requires.

Employee's View

Now we have started on a more productive course of analysis than merely asking a supervisor for characteristics. But we have only started. The picture we've sketched is one-dimensional, drawn only from the perspective of the supervisor. To test and refine the list of qualifications we are developing, we should get the same information from people who are currently performing the job by asking them to identify what they actually do on the job, and then analyzing what abilities, knowledge, or other characteristics these tasks require.

Why do we need to duplicate what we've already learned from the supervisor? The answer is because usually we don't duplicate. Instead, we learn that the tasks the supervisor *thinks* the employee is spending time on differ significantly from what the employee *in fact* spends time on. And even when the tasks turn out to be similar, the employer and the employee often differ on what characteristics are necessary to perform the task effectively.

Let's explore how those differences may occur by taking another example from the list of tasks identified above—produce reports within a short time period. To the supervisor, this task may require that an employee work long hours, perhaps staying up all night for two nights in a row. The employee, however, may see the necessary characteristics as quite different, perhaps requiring strong organizational skills, the foresight to assemble necessary personnel at the proper time, and the abilities to plan ahead and to work quickly.

Which of the two is correct in his assessment, the supervisor or the employee? Both, or neither. What's clear from this example is that there is a difference between what the job *requires* and how the job is *performed*. In the example above, the job required that reports be prepared in a short period of time. That task could be performed, however, in at least two widely divergent ways.

It's tempting for an employer to define a necessary job characteristic by reference to the way he imagines the job should be performed or by the way the job in fact has been performed by a particular employee. Doing either of those, however, may restrict the pool of candidates, eliminating people who can in fact meet the job requirements by performing a task in a different way. In some cases, it may also stand in the way of the job being performed in the most effective way.

Other Points of View and Sources

The combined analysis of the supervisor and the employee, while better than taking only the supervisor's point of view, may still lack valuable perspectives. Depending upon the job involved, it may be important to see the job through the eyes of other people in the company who, though not the employee's supervisors, are either consumers of the employee's services or coworkers. Where the employee has significant contacts outside of the company, with suppliers, customers, or others, it may be worth seeking those points of view, as well. By combining all of these perspectives, the employer can begin to assemble the most complete picture possible of the job.

Uh-oh, what's this "begin to assemble"? Does that mean there is more to this process? Alas, yes.

First of all, there are other sources of information you should look at. Review the performance-evaluation forms your company uses to assess people in this job. This may suggest additional characteristics you should consider. Presumably the characteristics you are looking for in a candidate are those being evaluated by the company in its performance reviews. If not, something's wrong. You may need to change your performance evaluation criteria.

Another source you should look to in developing and refining job characteristics is the profiles of those who either have been highly successful or have failed at your company. By looking at the characteristics that those who succeeded or failed possessed (or failed to possess), you should be able to better assess what characteristics are necessary to perform the job. You may analyze the characteristics of successful and unsuccessful people at the company either by reviewing performance-evaluation files, through interviews with those people or those who supervise them, or through some combination of the two. What you are looking for is those characteristics that distinguish outstanding performers from average or below-average performers. And the answers you get may surprise you.

One final source to look at is the characteristics necessary for successful performance by the employee at a higher level in the company. To the extent that you are hiring people for career positions, you should consider the prospects for them progressing over time. To determine the characteristics they will need, follow the same procedures you used to determine the characteristics for the current job.

Refining Your List

Let us assume now that you have completed the analysis suggested above and arrived at a list of well-defined characteristics you are looking for in candidates for the position. You may have produced an enormously long list of characteristics. For example, in my work with law firms, various firms identified the following characteristics they were looking for in their lawyers:

intelligence	flexibility
articulateness	maturity
aggressiveness	judgment
self-confidence	thoroughness
decisiveness	writing ability
creativity	personableness
organized	resourcefulness
analytical ability	foresight
ability to work with others	tough-mindedness

ability to deal with stress

common sense

self-starter

tolerance for routine tasks

character

attention to detail

entrepreneurial

enthusiasm

sense of humor

energy

motivation

 —defined goals

 —interest

 —competitiveness

assertiveness

reliable

perspective

depth

breadth

perceptiveness

leadership

hard working

productive

practicality

adaptability

honesty

original

Obviously, it would be impossible to identify whether a candidate possesses all of these characteristics in an interview. (On the other hand, it would be hard *not* to get a reading on some of these characteristics during the course of an interview, e.g., articulateness, personableness, maturity, self-confidence.)

One way of trying to get a better handle on the characteristics you are looking for is to group them in a way that makes sense to you. Consider, for example, the following groupings of the characteristics listed above (of course, many of these characteristics could fit into more than one group):

Professional Skills

intelligence

articulateness

decisiveness

creativity

analytical ability

thoroughness

judgment

organized

attention to detail

writing ability

resourcefulness

foresight

tolerance for routine tasks
perceptiveness
practicality

tough-mindedness
perspective
honesty

People Skills

work with others
common sense
character
deal with stress
leadership
depth
adaptability

maturity
flexibility
personableness
sense of humor
breadth
reliable

Motivation

self-starter
self-confidence
aggressiveness
energy
interest
hard working
preparation for interview

competitiveness
defined goals
entrepreneurial
enthusiasm
assertiveness
productivity

It's also important to recognize that since no candidate is likely to possess all of the characteristics you are looking for, you will need to prioritize those characteristics. One sensible way of doing that is to place the characteristics into categories. You might try the following four:

- essential to the job
- important, but not essential
- desirable
- a nice bonus

In determining which category to put characteristics into, you should consider the extent to which a particular characteristic can be acquired rather quickly or easily by a candidate once he starts work. Such a characteristic would be placed in a lower category than an equally important characteristic that would be much more difficult for an employee to acquire. This prioritization of characteristics will become important when we talk about how to make decisions, later in the book.

Recognize that, even as to characteristics you identify as essential to the job, not all those you hire will be equally strong in all those characteristics. Nor should they be. You need balance on your team (as long as each member has a threshold level of competence in essential areas).

Your Company's Climate

In determining the characteristics for any job, it is also important to consider the company's culture, the climate that exists within the firm that will affect a person's job performance. While there are many ways of looking at a company's climate, I find the approach developed by McBer & Company in Boston to be the most useful. McBer has determined that six elements of a company's climate are the primary factors affecting job performance:

1. *Conformity*—the degree to which a person is restrained by unnecessary rules and regulations.
2. *Responsibility*—the degree to which people are given responsibility for areas of their job performance.
3. *Standards*—the degree to which high standards are imposed upon employees within the organization and the organization itself.

4. *Rewards*—the extent to which a person perceives that his performance is rewarded by the company.
5. *Clarity*—the degree to which the employee understands what is expected of him and how that fits into the organization's goals.
6. *Team spirit*—the degree to which people are proud to be associated with the company.

Let's assume, for example, that you determine that your company is high in conformity—you have many rules and regulations, some of which may be quite unnecessary. Unless you have reason to believe that your company is going to get rid of those rules, you will need to hire people who can cope with this sort of rigidity. Should you find a talented but rebellious candidate, chances are she will not survive in your company's climate.

To take another example, suppose that your company is extremely hierarchical. Employees are not given much responsibility and are expected to report daily on almost every step they take. Hiring an entrepreneurial sort who likes to set his own course and sail it alone would be inviting disaster.

The style of managers in a company influences its climate. And an employee's success may depend upon her ability to adapt to the managerial style of her supervisor. Again, McBer identifies six managerial styles:

1. *Coercive*—the "do it the way I tell you" manager who closely controls subordinates and motivates by threats and discipline.
2. *Authoritative*—the firm but fair manager who gives subordinates clear direction and motivates by persuasion and feedback on task performance.
3. *Affiliative*—the "people first, task second" manager who emphasizes good personal relationships among

subordinates and motivates by trying to keep people happy with fringe benefits, security, and social activities.

4. *Democratic*—the participative manager who encourages subordinate input in decision making and motivates by rewarding team effort.

5. *Pace setting*—the "do it myself" manager who performs many tasks personally, expects a subordinate to follow his or her example, and motivates by setting high standards and letting subordinates work on their own.

6. *Coaching*—the developmental manager who helps and encourages subordinates to improve their performance, and motivates by providing opportunities for professional development.

As in the case of an organization's climate, the managerial style of your managers may affect your hiring decisions. For example, a highly independent candidate who likes to do things her own way would certainly not do well under a coercive manager, and probably would have trouble with a pace-setting manager, as well.

Of course, since managers may change, you should not give undue influence to the particular manager involved. In some circumstances, however, where the employee must work closely with a single, strong manager, that managerial style must be considered in determining whom you hire.

Analyzing your company's climate and the managerial styles of its managers takes both time and skill. For now, it is sufficient to alert you to the implications of these factors for your hiring decisions.

Watch for Changes

Finally, after all this analysis, note that the job you are filling may—indeed almost certainly will—change over time. If you doubt that, consider what tasks and skills used to be performed by, or required of, the position for which you are interviewing five years ago. Technological growth has made many skills that were once important obsolete, and has created a whole host of new skills necessary for many jobs.

The changing nature of most jobs today means you must hire somebody flexible enough to adapt to future changes that may occur. It also means you must reassess the characteristics you are looking for in a particular job category periodically.

Other Preparation for the Interview

Identifying the characteristics the interviewer is looking for is the most important, but not the only, preparation he must do for the interview. Other preparation should include the following:

- Practice. Somehow practicing interviewing skills has become acceptable for interviewees, but not for interviewers. The reason seems to go back to the old notion of assumed expertise—interviewers are supposed to know how to conduct an interview. To practice is to admit that you don't know everything. And that's embarrassing.

  Go ahead. Embarrass yourself. There's no better way to prepare for interviewing than to do a few practice interviews, and talk about them afterward. Ask the interviewee how she felt in the interview. If possible, have a third party watch the interview, either in the interview room, or better still, if you have the technological capability, from outside the room. Ask that third person to comment on what he observed. Videotape the session, and watch it again afterward.

If you are interviewing on university campuses, use students as practice interviewees. Or, if you hire students to work for you for the summer, ask them to serve as your guinea pigs. The students will learn something from the process, too. And, better still, they'll know that you value recruitment, and take it seriously.

- Before your interview, know what's already taken place with respect to the candidate. For example, interviewers at the company should assume that questions about grades and references from an interviewee's prior jobs have been resolved by the screening interviewer, and should not inquire into these subjects. Interviewees who are subjected repeatedly to questions about grades emerge from interviews feeling less positive about the company.
- Read the candidate's resume, twice—once well in advance of the interview, to prepare a plan for the interview, and once immediately prior to the interview to refresh your recollection.
- Develop a plan for the interview. This need not—indeed, should not—be a detailed schedule of how you will spend each minute of the interview. Rather, it should be an outline of which aspects of the candidate's qualifications you intend to explore in most depth, and how. In order to do that, you will have to:
  —have a clear understanding of what characteristics are most important for the job.
  —review the candidate's resume to assess which of those characteristics you believe are most and least

likely to be present in the candidate. For example, if a resume indicated that a candidate had formed his own lawn-care business in high school and had been elected president of his college class, you might hypothesize that he was a motivated, self-starter with entrepreneurial, people, and leadership skills.

—identify a few aspects of the candidate's resume that you intend to explore in the interview. For example, if the resume referred to above had no mention of academic awards, grade point average, or class rank, you might decide to explore the candidate's intellectual ability and attention to detail, if those were important to the job. (Interviewees beware: If you do not mention academic or other achievements, interviewers will assume that you have not earned them.)

—have in mind what information you want to gather during the interview particularly if you are the first interviewer. This may include: the candidate's academic performance, names and phone numbers of references, the candidate's interests and general concerns (geographical location, compensation, opportunities for advancement, etc.), specific concerns the candidate may have about your company and information (such as outside interests) that will allow you to judge who in your company the candidate may match up well with if you invite her to come for additional interviews.

—understand what aspects of the candidate's background, if any, have already been explored or are to be explored by other people who will be interviewing the candidate. Look at the interview schedule and try to figure out what perspectives you can add to that of others on the list.

• If the candidate is a student or a recent graduate, know

something about his school, its grading system and the honors it awards. This will show the candidate you care about what you are doing and will also avoid wasting valuable interview time asking about these matters.

- Know your company and its reputation. Chances are that many candidates will have reviewed available literature produced by your company. You should have reviewed that material, as well. And not cursorily, six months ago, but thoroughly and recently. Similarly, if there are recent newspaper or magazine articles about your company, you should have read them.

  If you're interviewing a candidate from a university or graduate program, you should also be aware of your company's reputation on the interviewee's campus. Your reputation is likely to vary from one campus to another. Being aware of that reputation will give you a better sense of what the candidate is likely to think of your company and should help you to anticipate and prepare for questions the interviewee may raise.

- Know what your company has to sell the candidate. Review chapters 10 and 11, "Selling Yourself or Your Company" and "Identifying and Handling Obstacles," to refresh your recollection on how most effectively to sell and deal with the problems you may encounter.

- Clear your schedule, desk, and mind before the interview. If you are thinking about other tasks you have to perform that day, you will not devote the attention you need to the interview. If you are interviewing on campus, do not try to transact business during breaks in your interview schedule. Instead, use those breaks to see faculty members, visit with the placement director, review your company's file in the placement office, look at competing companies' sign-up lists or contact students you have seen in prior years or who have worked with you during the summer.

- Allow plenty of time for the interview.
- Periodically, review the interviewer tips and techniques contained in this book.

If preparation seems like a formidable task, that's because it is. But it also happens to be crucial to conducting an effective interview and to avoiding the interview game. Without preparation, the interview becomes an aimless conversation.

Fortunately, there are payoffs for all of your preparation. Determining the job-related characteristics you are looking for will help you to avoid illegal-hiring practices that arise when you ask questions unrelated to the job's requirements. Hiring the right people means you will be getting employees who become productive more quickly. And it also means that you will reduce the enormous financial and personal costs of high turnover. So don't shortcut the preparation process.

TWO

PREPARING FOR THE INTERVIEW:
Interviewee

One curse of being a parent is that your children don't ask you for advice. The beauty of being a writer, though, is that sometimes you can give it to them anyway.

In thinking about how I might most usefully offer interviewees some advice about preparing for the interview process—in other words, how to inflict a little wisdom on you—it struck me that I might best do that by imagining it was one of my daughters seeking that advice. That would assure that I was trying to provide counsel that would be both sound and sensitive. It would also explain why this chapter might sound a bit paternalistic. So, here goes. (Don't be misled by the fact that this advice sounds as if it's being given to a younger, first-time job seeker, though. The same counsel applies to older persons who may have worked for some time.)

You're Not Alone

You say you're a little frightened, not sure what to expect? You feel as if you're putting yourself out on the line, that people will be evaluating your worth? You're concerned you may be rejected, and not sure what that rejection will say about you? Some of your friends are out interviewing, too. And what will you say to them if you are not offered a job? You say this job-interview stuff seems very important and serious, almost life and death?

Would it surprise you to know that almost every interviewee who ever interviewed for a job has had those feelings at one time or another? Of course, that doesn't mean the feelings you have aren't real, or that you don't need to deal with them. You do. But perhaps you can take a little comfort in knowing you aren't alone; far from it.

First off, you should recognize that those feelings you're having aren't all bad. Being a little nervous and excited will get you "up" for the interview. As an old interviewer, I can tell you that there are few things an interviewer dreads more than encountering an interviewee who seems bored, like she's just going through the motions. That bit of nervousness and excitement you're feeling is what gets the adrenaline flowing, and it may help you do your best. If you don't believe me, ask any athlete or actor.

Controlling Jitters

Experienced interviewers expect a bit of nervousness early on in an interview (for example, a slight quaver in your voice), and they ignore it. On the other hand, too much fright will certainly get in your way. It will prevent you from focusing on what you need to do in the interview. So how do you maintain some balance, arrive at the optimum level of nervousness?

One reason you're nervous is because you don't know what to expect. Reading this book should help. Pay particular attention to the mistakes interviewers make. Chances are good that the people who interview you will fall into many of those same traps. By being aware of the pitfalls, you will be less uncomfortable when they occur and you may even help your interviewers avoid them.

There's a big difference, though, between knowing what to expect and developing the comfort that you can handle what you will encounter. The latter comes only from experience. So find a way to practice. Ask somebody—a relative, a friend, a teacher—to interview you. If you are fortunate enough to know somebody involved in interviewing and hiring people for a company, try to get that person to act as your interviewer.

Conduct the practice interview in a context as close to a real interview situation as you can. Give the interviewer your resume. Tell him to assume that he has never met you and knows only what is on your resume. Conduct the interview in a place you are not familiar with. Play it straight. Don't laugh and joke as you do it.

After the interview is over, discuss it with your interviewer. Ask him to be brutally frank about your performance. Get suggestions as to what might have improved your presentation. This type of postinterview debriefing is important. Remember that once you start doing real interviews you will almost never get direct, honest feedback on what might have improved your interview performance. Take advantage of the opportunity to get that feedback now, when you can.

Don't rely solely on your interviewer's comments. Make your own notes on the interview. What would you have done or said differently? Is there anything you forgot to say or ask about? (Use this note taking after your real interviews start, too.)

Then do it all over again. Find another person who will conduct a practice interview with you, and then debrief you afterward. If you can find a third person, do it yet again. The more you practice, the more comfortable you will feel in your real interviews.

Your goal is to become relaxed, but you don't want to go overboard. The interview has a certain formality that amounts to an interview etiquette. Violating that etiquette will be viewed by an interviewer in the same way she would view your eating spaghetti with your fingers at an interview lunch. So, although you want to be able to talk comfortably with the interviewer, you don't want to start off by slumping down into your chair, putting your feet up on the interviewer's desk and saying, "So what shall we talk about, Herb old boy?"

The need to conduct practice interviews applies not only to people who are looking for their first job, but also to those who find themselves back in the market after a number of years. Just because you have worked for several years, that is no reason you should feel a greater comfort level in the interview. Indeed, the opposite may be true. The interview may be more important to you. The job is probably at a much higher level. And, having been out of the job market for some time, you may be less familiar with the interview process.

If you have access to videotape facilities for your practice interviews, by all means take advantage of that. By reviewing your interview video you will notice things about the way you present yourself—your voice, the way you look, nervous habits you may have, your posture—that you would not otherwise be aware of. Seeing yourself on video can be painful, but subjecting yourself to that short-term pain will provide long-term benefits in your interviewing performance.

Who Am I?

Before you go into your practice interview, ask yourself, "What am I looking for?" But before you do that, ask yourself an even more basic question, namely, "Who am I?" Of course, many people spend a lifetime asking themselves that question. I do not believe that going through a four-year psychoanalysis is a necessary prerequisite for a job interview. But it doesn't hurt. What I am suggesting here, though, is a somewhat less ambitious inquiry into who you are, insofar as that question affects your job choice.

There are a number of ways of approaching this inquiry. Ask yourself questions such as:

What do I enjoy doing?
What gives me the greatest satisfaction?
What do I not enjoy doing?
What are my strengths?
What are my weaknesses?
What is my self-image; how do I envision myself?
What motivates me?
Of all the things I've done, what am I proudest of?
What are my goals, both short-term and long-term?
What type of job would allow me to achieve those goals?

Take the time to actually sit down and write out your answers to these questions. Unless you do, you are unlikely to reach more than rather superficial, incomplete answers. Nor will you be able to detect patterns or inconsistencies between your answers.

Once you've written them out, discuss your answers with any friends, family members, or advisers who could provide guidance. This process should help you to define the characteristics of positions for which you are best suited, positions that would be most likely to provide you the greatest long-term satisfaction. Since people generally perform best when they like what they are doing, this process should also help identify positions in which you would perform well.

Make sure that your goals are realistic, though. I recall a *Wall Street Journal* cartoon in which an interviewer, looking down at a resume, remarks, "I notice that one of your long-term goals is world conquest."

Identify Types of Jobs

Once you've answered the who-am-I questions, your next step is to gather information about what types of jobs require or encourage your strengths, what you enjoy doing, what gives you satisfaction. Use whatever sources are available to you—friends, relatives, placement directors, career counselors, libraries, job fairs—to compile as complete a list as possible. Start out with a broad range of choices; you can always narrow the list later. Armed with that list, you can begin to match your strengths and desires with what's available in the job market to assess which positions best fit your needs and abilities.

Assessing Job Characteristics

After you have determined the type of a position you should be seeking, begin to ask yourself questions regarding which aspects of a job are important to you. These may include the following:

> salary
> prestige
> benefits
> hours
> flexibility
> training
> people you work with
> level of responsibility
> geographical location
> physical office environment
> intellectual challenge
> opportunity for advancement
> job security

Be sure to take account of any practical, absolute limitations on your accepting a position. For example, are you available to work only certain hours? Must you be in a certain area of the country? Is there a minimum salary you must earn? It makes no more sense for you to waste time considering positions that do not meet your minimum criteria than it would for an employer to linger over a candidate who did not meet the basic skill requirements for a job.

Once you have identified the job characteristics you are looking for, try to prioritize them. Focus on those that would make a job most rewarding to you. Discount factors that would prove only minor or temporary inconveniences. As with interviewers, this prioritization will become important when we discuss decision making.

Obviously, the importance you place on some of the job characteristics listed above will differ depending on whether you are looking for a temporary job or for something that may be longer term. Opportunity for advancement, of course, would not be relevant for a temporary position. Also, your analysis is likely to vary depending upon whether this is an entry-level job or a position you are seeking later in your career. For example, training might not be very important for a person coming into a senior position.

The analysis I am suggesting here is not easy. To do it right will require considerable time and introspection. If you have not tried to ask and answer these questions, though, your success in finding the right job will prove purely a matter of luck, or trial and error. (Remember Yogi Berra.) Of course, to some extent, luck and trial and error *will* come into play in job selection over your lifetime. But you need not, and should not, entrust the job-seeking process solely to those fickle and inefficient forces.

Other Preparation

Once you have completed the analysis of who you are and what you are looking for, there are other preparatory steps you should take prior to the interview, similar to those identified in chapter 1 for an employer. Those would include:

- Learn whatever you can about the company you are interviewing with and the industry that company is in. Depending on the company, you can get that information from public sources such as newspapers, magazines, or required public filings with federal, state, or local regulatory agencies, or directly from the company itself (simply by calling and asking. Do not be afraid to indicate why you are asking for the information. Even if a person who will be interviewing you learns that you have called to request information, she will most likely be impressed by the initiative you have taken.).

Interviewers consider interviewees who fail to learn what they can about a company from readily available material as showing a lack of serious interest in the company. It also may be viewed as an indication that you do not prepare adequately for a task, a characteristic the interviewer may assume will apply on the job, as well. Typically, failure to learn about the company is telegraphed by your asking questions that are answered in company brochures, or making comments that indicate you have not read that material.

When you have researched the company, though, don't feel you have to force all the information you learn into the interview. For example, saying, "I happened to notice that your sales revenues increased 4.2 percent in the last two years and that net after-tax earnings, after allowing for special adjustments, increased 6.84 percent. That's very good." would be taken by an interviewer as showing off. On the other hand, asking, "Do you expect your recent rate of increased earnings to continue this year?" would be appropriate. Remember that the primary purpose of gathering information about a company is to inform you, not to impress the interviewer.

- Learn what you can about the interviewer if you know who he will be. This will be more difficult than getting information about the company, but you may be able to learn something by asking another interviewer who has already interviewed you, or by asking your prospective interviewer's secretary.

There may be other sources, as well. I recall one candidate who particularly impressed me. Between the time he wrote to me and I wrote back asking him to give me a call, Tom had determined that one of his former law professors and I had coauthored an article

some ten years earlier. He'd done that simply by looking for my name in an index to legal periodicals. Tom
later became my law partner, and brought the same
thorough approach to resolving client problems as he
did to his own job search.

Seeking information about your interviewers does
carry some risk. You will want to do it tactfully, and
in moderation. You won't want to come across as if
you were the FBI (unless, perhaps, you are applying
for a job with an investigative agency).

- Allow plenty of time for the interview. Scheduling interviews so that you have to rush off to another appointment will brand you as discourteous, not important. To
avoid this problem, find out before you interview how
long you will be expected to be at the company.
- Clear your mind of other matters before the interview.
- Have in mind what characteristics about yourself you
would like to get across in the interview. Review everything you've done in the past for evidence of these
characteristics. You may have done some things that
will be impressive to an interviewer that you have taken
for granted.
- Review each item on your resume to consider whether
an interviewer is likely to ask about it, and why. Formulate some messages and information you would want
to convey for each entry. Be prepared to address weak
spots or gaps in your resume if there are any.
- Have in mind questions that are important for you to
get answered at this stage in the interview process.
- If this is a second-round interview with the company,
recognize that the first interviewer you saw in your
screening interview must have liked you. Make that
interviewer your ally and mentor for future interviews.
Don't hesitate to call that person for advice or with

questions. Do this in moderation, however. Generally, one call is enough. If you make too many calls, you may convert your ally into an opponent, making her wonder why she ever liked you in the first place.

- Periodically review the tips for interviewees contained in this book.

Putting the Interview into Perspective

Now I know that not even all of the preparation I've suggested is going to make you totally comfortable. That's because, quite aside from the effect of not knowing what to expect in the interview, you are nervous because of what the job interview means to you. This is it. Real life. Your future. Your career. What you'll be doing for the rest of your life. Success and failure hang in the balance.

Wait a minute, let's try to put this into some kind of perspective. Almost nobody stays in one job anymore. The days of your grandparents, when a person went to a company and stayed there for life, are over. Chances are good that the job you are interviewing for will occupy your time for only a couple of years, maybe less. That's not to say it's unimportant. But it's a far cry from determining your future. Imagining that it does will only increase the pressure you feel in interviewing to an unrealistic and undesirable level.

And remember, we're not even talking about the job yet, we're just talking about an interview. What's the worst thing that can come out of the interview? That you are not made a job offer? Actually, that may be the best thing that could come out of the interview. Chances are you will interview for quite a number of positions in which you would not be happy.

Remember that the interviewer is not judging your worth as a human being. The fact that he or she does not offer you the job is not a reflection on you. You are not a bad or a lesser person because of it. If the interview is conducted correctly, and you do not receive an offer, it may mean only that you and the position are not a good match.

But let's assume you run into an interviewer who has not had the good sense to read this book. Because of that egregious error, he conducts an interview that does not allow him to recognize that you would be a perfect person for the position he is seeking to fill. Instead of doing what any sensible interviewer would have done—make you an offer—this person writes you one of those letters that thanks you for coming in, tells you how much he enjoyed meeting you, compliments you on your fine record—and then tells you to get lost (though he probably wishes you, and may even predict, "success in your future career").

So what's happened? You've gotten a bad break. You've missed out on an opportunity that might have been a good one for you. But is it the end of the world? Heck no, far from it. Are you less of a candidate because of it? Not a bit. Remember, it was the *interviewer's* mistake. Think of his poor company, who will be deprived of your services because of his failing. Too bad for them.

Keep in mind that there is a good deal of luck involved in interviewing. Whether you get an offer may depend on whether you and the interviewer have something in common; on the timing of when your application landed (somebody may have resigned just the day before); or on whether you or the interviewer are having a good or bad day. Do not expect more rationality from the interview process than is reasonable.

Being an interviewee is character-building. You are going to get rejected. You're going to be disappointed. Count on it. Quite likely, often. But it's good practice for the rejection and disappointment you're going to find inevitably (but I hope not too often) no matter what job you land. So, in that respect, the interview process is good preparation for any position, and for real life.

Come up with ways of dealing with rejection so that it will not affect your performance in subsequent interviews. I know of one interviewee who explicitly rejected rejection, writing the following letter to interviewers:

> Dear Ms. ———:
> Thank you very much for your letter of 18 October 1989. Your kind words and enthusiasm are both impressive and appreciated.
> I have now had the opportunity to review your letter with members of my rejection committee. I regret that I am unable to accept your rejection. This decision was a difficult one to make, but because of my limited ability to deal with rejection I cannot accept such letters from all of the qualified interviewers that I meet.
> On the strength of your discussions with me and your literary skills, I am certain that you will find many who will be willing to accommodate your rejection needs. Thank you for your interest and your prompt attention.
> Very truly yours,

Look at interviewing as an adventure. As with any adventure, there'll be unexpected surprises. Expect that. Consider interviewing an opportunity to learn—about various companies you'll speak to, about some interesting people you're likely to meet as interviewers, and about yourself. Use your interviews as a way to hone some skills that are going to stand you in good stead in whatever job you land—the ability to present yourself well, to carry on a conversation with a person in a position of some power over you, to listen attentively, to analyze the pros and cons of a situation, and to develop your self-confidence. In other words, treat the interview seriously, but not so seriously that you can't enjoy yourself.

A Postscript: Learning from the Other Side

Interviewers and interviewees can each benefit from understanding what the other should do in preparation for the interview. At a minimum, that understanding should provide both parties an appreciation for the difficulty of that preparation, and a certain empathy for the other's task. Beyond that, though, understanding the necessary preparation for the other side of the table should suggest fruitful areas of inquiry for you in your current role. For example, an interviewee in exploring a job possibility may consider questions such as:

- Has the interviewer really defined the characteristics he is looking for?
- In what aspects of the job are those characteristics necessary?
- Are there other ways of doing the job that may enhance the value of my strengths? (If, for example, the interviewer believes the job requires an aggressive, confrontational style, can I show him how I have used a low-key, team-oriented approach to achieve results in similar situations?)
- Do I have not only the characteristics necessary to be hired into this position, but also those necessary to advance to a higher level?
- What are the characteristics that distinguish an outstanding performer in this position, and do I possess them?

An interviewer, on the other hand, may wish to consider the following:

- To what extent has the interviewee analyzed the questions suggested in this chapter?

- What does this preparation/lack of preparation suggest about the interviewee?
- Which elements of a job are most important for the interviewee?
- What does that suggest about the interviewee's likely performance on the job?
- Does the job I have to offer suit the interviewee's job-selection criteria?

Finally, understanding the necessary preparation from the other side of the table may allow you to help the other person undertake that preparation, after the interview. And that effort may benefit not only you, but future generations of interviewers and interviewees as well.

THREE

IN THE BEGINNING: Creating a Comfortable Interview Setting

Once you've prepared for the interview, you're almost ready to begin. But before you do, let's take a look at the structure of an interview. Though an interview should have three sections—the opening, the body, and the close—an experienced interviewer will make the three parts appear seamless. Each section is discussed in detail elsewhere, but here they are, in brief:

1. *The opening* The purpose of this portion is to make the interviewee feel comfortable, to set the stage for a productive exchange of information in the balance of the interview. In a half-hour interview, this introduction should take approximately three minutes. Try to make a smooth transition from the opening to the next section of the interview. For example, "Now I'd like to ask you some questions about your work experience" is definitely preferable to, "That's about enough idle chitchat, let's get on with the interview."

2. *The body of the interview* This consists of an evaluation of the candidate, information gathering for use in future interviews and indirect selling of the company, primarily through the interviewer showing a real interest in the candidate. This portion of the interview should take at least twenty minutes in a half-hour interview. Again, consider a smooth transition to the close, such as, "I've enjoyed learning more about you. We have a few minutes left for any questions you may have about the company."

3. *The close* This portion should include a brief opportunity for questions, thanking the interviewee for coming to interview and explaining when and how the interviewee will hear from the company. Any overt selling of the company should be done during the closing of the interview, generally in response to a candidate's questions. This portion should take approximately five minutes in a half-hour interview. A common mistake is to allow too much time for this portion of the interview.

Establishing a Comfort Level

It's important to recognize up front that the interview is an artificial construct. Why do I say that? Well, outside of an interview, how often are two complete strangers locked in a room alone together for half an hour or so, each seeking desperately to make a favorable impression on the other while at the same time trying to pry as much information as they can out of the other? Neither party is likely to feel at ease in that situation.

Why is being at ease important? In the interview, each party is trying to get information from, and convey information to, the other. But what happens when you are talking to somebody and do not feel at ease? You naturally turn defensive, clam up, and don't give the other person the information he wants—or you give him *only* the information he asks for, and you certainly do not volunteer any additional information. And an anxious interviewer or interviewee is unlikely to pay full attention to what the other has to say. In short, unless they feel at ease, both parties tend to revert to playing the interview game, which provides them with the comfort of predictable rules and the prospect of no surprises.

Let's consider what may be going through each person's mind as an interview begins? The interviewer may be thinking: Who is this person I'm talking to? Why doesn't he just go away and let me get back to the project I need to finish? How am I ever going to finish all of the things I need to do at work today? What questions am I going to ask? What questions *can't* I ask, or I'll get in trouble? I have to remember to get to the cleaners before they close tonight, and to let the Johnsons know we're not going to make it for dinner Saturday night.

The interviewee, for his part, may be thinking: Who is this person I'm talking to? Will she be the one who decides whether or not I'm offered this job? I have to get back right after this interview to finish up that work that's due tomorrow. Is my hair combed right? I hope Sally can go to that play on Friday.

In addition, the interviewee is likely to feel:

> nervous
> insecure
> defensive
> anxious to make a favorable impression
> that this interview is a lifetime decision

Of course, not every interviewee will feel exactly the same way. An interviewee's feelings will be affected by the experience she has had in interviewing, the degree of success achieved so far in school or work, whether she already has other offers, the urgency of getting a job soon, and the desirability of the particular job. Nonetheless, the above feelings are surprisingly applicable to a great many interviewees. Indeed, experienced interviewers often marvel at the insecurity of even the most outstanding candidates.

In other words, both the interviewer and the interviewee may have a lot of other things on their minds. They may have anxieties, both relating to the interview situation and outside of it.

Getting Off on the Right Foot

It's up to the interviewer to get the interview off to a good start. Unless she does this in the first few minutes of the interview, chances are good that the interview will never get on track.

And remember that the climate you establish in the interview will affect your chances of attracting the interviewee to your company. A candidate will assume that the atmosphere you create in the interview mirrors what he will find when he arrives at the company. So treat the interviewee as a guest (or a client or customer), not as an adversary.

To get off to that good start, the interviewer must take cognizance of how the interviewee seems to be feeling: attempt to understand why the interviewee might feel that way; analyze the extent to which these feelings could help the interviewer to achieve his goals; and identify ways of neutralizing or eliminating the feelings that will interfere with achieving his goals. That sounds like a daunting task. Fortunately, though, experienced interviewers do most of this automatically. Here are some specific approaches you may use to get the interview off to a good start:

1. Don't keep the interviewee waiting. Doing that is saying to him, "Your time is not worth anything; mine is."

   An interviewee should also be on time. Being late will be taken as a sign of rudeness and lack of interest in the position. (The exception to this rule is the true story of an interviewee who showed up twenty minutes late for an interview explaining that his luggage had been lost on the plane and so he'd stopped to purchase a suit at a nearby store.) On the other hand, don't show up too early as that may annoy the interviewer.

2. Meet the interviewee at the door of your office, or pick him up in the reception area. This small effort shows you are willing to meet the interviewee half-way, and that you respect and value him. This will make the interviewee far more comfortable than he would be were he first to encounter you ensconced behind your desk. If you begin your conversation on the way back to your office or desk, you may be able to introduce a certain relaxed informality into the interview.

3. Smile, look the interviewee in the eye, shake hands. A warm greeting, without ever saying a word, can help greatly to relax the interviewee.

   Handshakes and eye contact ARE important, for both parties. (Some old saws just happen to be true.) Your handshake is practically your first contact—and your only physical contact—with the other person. A firm handshake projects strength, self-confidence, and determination. Maintaining eye contact projects honesty, sincerity, and confidence. Limp handshakes and shifting eyes or downward glances tend to project the opposite of these characteristics. The other person may be able to get beyond those stereotypes, but do you really want to dig yourself into that hole?

4. Invite the interviewee to sit down, and indicate where you wish him to sit. This may seem like a rather insignificant point. After all, even if not invited to do so, most interviewees will sit, eventually. The reason for mentioning it is that even a brief, awkward moment early in the interview can affect the interviewee's comfort level.

   Indeed, failure to indicate where to sit may affect the interviewer's comfort level, too. A hiring partner friend of mine told me of a time as a law student when he interviewed with a partner who had a rather unusual office configuration. It wasn't until the interview was over and the interviewer came around to look in his desk drawer that my friend realized he was sitting in the interviewer's desk chair. I suspect my friend got high marks for assertiveness, at least until he blubbered his apologies when he realized what he'd done.

   If you are comfortable in doing so and your office arrangement permits it, do not interview from behind your desk. The desk becomes a physical and psychological barrier to establishing a relationship with the interviewee.

5. Introduce yourself and tell the interviewee briefly who you are and what your position is in the company. Every interviewee is curious about the person he is talking to. You know something about the interviewee by virtue of having read his resume. Telling something about yourself will help to level the field. (But beware of leveling the field by introducing

yourself, the job and the company for half the interview. Aside from the time problem, telling the interviewee too much about the job and the company early on allows him to shape his interests and characteristics to fit the description you've given.)

6. Ask the interviewee what he likes to be called. Don't assume you know the answer. For example, if the interviewee's name is Alfred Jones, calling him "Mr. Jones" is going to set a formal (and perhaps artificial) tone to the interview. And if you try to call him by his first name, you will not know whether he goes by Alfred, Al, Fred, Alfie, or even A. J. Calling the interviewee by a name he is not used to being called may make him extremely uncomfortable and adversely affect his performance. And yet, because of his own nervousness, he may not make the effort to correct you. Once you know what to call the interviewee, you may want to use the name a few times (but not every sentence) during the interview. Hearing one's name tends to make you feel more comfortable.

An interviewee should not call an interviewer by her first name, unless invited to do so. This is especially true in an initial interview in which the interviewer may view this behavior as inappropriately informal. This rule would not necessarily hold in follow-up interviews at the company, especially when the person you are speaking with is approximately your age. If you are in doubt as to what to call the interviewer, you may either ask what the interviewer would like to be called, use Mr. or Ms., or not use any name at all. Female interviewers should not be referred to as Miss or Mrs., because many women would be offended by either of those. In any case, try to remember the names of the people with whom you interview because you may have occasion to refer to those people at a later time.

7. Make sure the interviewee is comfortable physically. Don't smoke; don't even ask the interviewee whether he minds if you smoke. Is the sun shining in the interviewee's eyes? If it's warm in the office, would he like to take his coat off? Would he like something to drink? Does he need to go to the washroom? Tending to these sorts of concerns shows the interviewee that you are considering his needs as a real, live human being. Failure to do so may create an unintentionally stressful situation.

8. You may choose to explain to the interviewee how the interview is going to be conducted and, if he does not already know, how long the interview will last. For example, you may say, "I'd like to learn as much as I can about you during the half hour we have, so if you don't mind, I have some questions that I'd like to ask you. I know you may have some questions, too, and I plan to leave a bit of time toward the end of the interview for you to ask those questions."

Depending upon how comfortable you are with the concept, you may even want to discuss getting beyond the interview game directly with an interviewee. That discussion might go something like this:

INTERVIEWER: I suppose you've been through quite a few of these interviews.

INTERVIEWEE: Yes, I sure have.

INTERVIEWER: So have I. Sometimes I feel like they are all pretty much the same, it's as if we're both playing a game. You know, us inter-

INTERVIEWEE: viewers all asking the same questions and you interviewees trying to come up with the answers that you think we expect.

INTERVIEWEE: Yes, I feel that way myself sometimes.

INTERVIEWER: I'm going to do my best to avoid falling into that pattern. And the way I'm going to try to do that is to ask you questions about you and your experience, rather than the types of questions I might ask of just about anybody. I'd like to find out as much as I can about *you*. And I hope that you'll be as candid as possible in your answers, because I think what we're both really trying to do is to see whether there is a good fit between what you are interested in and good at doing and what we at my company have to offer. I'll try to talk candidly about the company, too, if you have any questions for me toward the end of the interview. Does that sound like a sensible approach?

INTERVIEWEE: It sure does. In fact, I'm sort of looking forward to this interview.

My purpose is not to script something out for you, but to suggest how you might approach being candid with an interviewee about the interview game. If an approach like this (or some other approach you devise) feels comfortable to you, you might try it. If it doesn't work, you can always drop it.

Setting the ground rules for the interview will make the interviewee more comfortable. Indeed, if you are the first person to see an interviewee who will be spending a day or half day at your company, you should explain what is planned for the day, including:

—the length of the interview day and the individual interviews

—luncheon plans

—who the interviewee will see, perhaps handing him a list of biographical information about those people

—that things may go awry during the course of the day

—mechanics, such as handling of expenses, etc.

9. Try to establish rapport with the interviewee. Some interviewers do this by acknowledging some of the difficulties of the interview situation. For example, in an on-campus interview situation, you might say, "I'm sure you've had a lot of interviews by now, and you realize how artificial it can get from both sides of the table. I'd like to see if we can get beyond that so I can really learn something about you in the short time we have together." Or, toward the end of a day of interviews at the company, you may say, "I'm sure you must be getting a little tired, and probably have been asked many of the same things over and over. So perhaps we could talk about something you haven't discussed earlier today."

10. Compliment the interviewee on some aspect of her resume, or on her resume in general. For example, "You've performed exceptionally well in school. That's terrific. Congratulations." Or, "You've done some really fascinating things, and I'm interested in talking to you about some of them." This type of compliment to the interviewee, if you mean it sincerely, is likely to make her feel good about herself and therefore cause her to relax.

11. Where the interviewee's resume indicates you have something in common with him, you may want to begin the interview by acknowledging that common

bond. For example, "I see you went to the University of Wisconsin as an undergraduate. I went there myself. Do they still . . . ?" Or, "I see you like to read. I'm an avid reader myself. What sort of books do you like to read?"

12. Another way of establishing rapport is to ask about something of particular interest to the interviewee as shown by her resume, even if it is something that you have no particular background in yourself. If you take this approach, try to show a sincere interest by asking more than just one question on the topic. For example, consider an interview that started as follows:

"I see that you are interested in breeding dogs. What kind of dogs do you breed?"
"Poodles."
"I see. And what courses did you take when you majored in history in college?"

This type of beginning would not show any real concern about the interviewee's interest in breeding dogs. Often, interviewers make the mistake of touching only superficially on a candidate's interests out of a concern for not consuming too much time in small talk. Obviously, you would not want to take up the entire interview with dog-breeding questions. But you can ask a surprising number of questions in a brief time. And there may be interviews in which you need to devote somewhat more than two or three minutes to breaking the ice. When an interviewee appears particularly nervous, another minute or two of small talk may relax her and make the rest of the interview more productive.

Be careful of your choice of icebreaking topics.

For example, some women object to a discussion of sports when there is nothing on their resume to indicate that interest. They may regard that as sexist, thus creating a mood quite different from what you'd hoped for in trying to break the ice. Indeed, in an exceptional circumstance when it's clear that the interview has gotten off to a bad start, you may even want to acknowledge that and start the interview over.

13. Don't begin the interview by discussing a prior job experience that is closely related to the job the interviewee is applying for. For example, when I was interviewing law students for a position as a new attorney with my firm, I never began the interview with a discussion of a summer job they may have had with another law firm. That type of closely related job experience is likely to be the most threatening thing you can discuss and therefore unlikely to cause the interviewee to relax and open up. Save this type of a discussion for later in the interview.

14. Adapt to the interviewee's pace. People have different speaking patterns with which they are most comfortable. If the interviewee is a slow or fast talker, try to adjust your pace to conform to his, rather then vying with him for control of the interview speed.

Some authors advise that you go beyond this and adopt the same posture as the other person and attune yourself to the type of imagery—physical, auditory, or visual—that a person uses and mimic that style yourself. For example if an interviewee uses visual phrases such as, "I see what you are getting at," or, "that looks good to me," you may use the phrase such as, "if you can picture this . . ."

To me, this comes too close to playing an interview game, if you *see* what I mean.

15. Avoid interruptions. Generally, this is not as much a problem on campus as it is back at the company. Have your calls held during an interview. Taking each call that comes in signals to an interviewee that she is the least important part of your day. Telling somebody to hold your calls shows just the opposite. If you know ahead of time you may have to take a brief, important call, tell the interviewee that at the outset. If you will have to take a long call, try to reschedule the interview.

If, as interviewee, you encounter an interviewer who permits interruptions in the form of phone calls or people coming into her office, try to take advantage of those interruptions. Listen to what is being said and, if appropriate, utilize what you have learned when the interview resumes. This will show the interviewer you are somebody with initiative, who uses his time well.

The Interviewee Can Help

Though it is primarily the interviewer's responsibility to set a relaxed tone for the interview, the interviewee can help, as well. An inexperienced interviewer may be even more nervous than the interviewee.

Where the interviewer has not used some of the suggestions listed above, the interviewee may adopt any of them himself. For example, at the end of an interview day on campus, one interviewee brought me a cup of coffee. That signaled to me that the interviewee understood my position as an interviewer, and might empathize with clients or co-workers. A friend told me of the interviewee who arrived for his last interview of the day with two cold beers in hand. Of course, this approach has its limits. My friend appreciated the beer, but the student did not receive an offer. Perhaps her mistake was trying to sell my friend the beer (only kidding).

If an interviewer has not attended to your physical comforts and you feel uncomfortable, don't hesitate to change your seat to avoid the sun, ask permission to take your jacket off, or request coffee or a soft drink. That will demonstrate self-assurance and assertiveness on your part. And, for heaven's sake, don't be afraid to take a break to go to the washroom. Most employers recognize this as a legitimate candidate need.

A smile and warm greeting from the interviewee may do as much to relax the interviewer as a smile from the interviewer will do to relax the interviewee. If you are interviewing in the company's offices, recognize that in all probability your interview is interrupting some work the interviewer is in the midst of doing. That means the interviewer may need a short time to get into the flow of the interview.

Also, when you are in an interviewer's office, it's a good idea to observe what is around the office. Does the interviewer have interesting artwork? Does she have photographs that may reveal particular interests of hers? Are there plaques, trophies, or diplomas that may give you information about her? Any of these observations may be a way for you to establish rapport with the interviewer or to compliment the interviewer on something. (Beware of giving compliments, though, since they may easily come across as insincere or obsequious. Save them for when you are truly enthusiastic about whatever you are complimenting the interviewer about.)

Team Interviews

Before the interview begins, the employer will need to decide whether to use one interviewer at a time, or more. Is it a good idea for employers to conduct team interviews in which two people from the company interview a candidate at the same time? The answer is—yes and no.

In general, a bad team interview tends to be worse than a bad one-on-one interview. But a good team interview can be at least as good as a one-on-one interview, and can accomplish a number of other purposes for the company.

A good team interview provides the following advantages:

- It's easier on interviewers, since they can permit someone else to take the lead and relax. That is especially important on campus, when many interviews follow in succession.
- It gives the company two judgments on each interviewee.
- It provides two people with whom the interviewee may be able to establish rapport.
- It provides two familiar faces who may be available to see the interviewee in later interviews.
- It may be an effective training technique for the less experienced interviewer in the team.
- It provides two people who can follow up with the interviewee if an offer is made.
- In the unfortunate event that a claim of discriminatory interviewing is made, it provides two people from the company to attest to what was said.

At the same time, a poorly conducted team interview will be terribly uncomfortable for the interviewee, and unproductive for the company. Besides the other disadvantages of a poor team interview, it is expensive for the company because it consumes two interviewers' time.

A bad team interview usually takes one of two forms. Too often, the team interview degenerates into an interrogation. The interviewee is bombarded by one question after another from different interviewers, being bounced back and forth like a Ping-Pong ball. The interviewee leaves feeling as if he had been a suspect for the heinous crime of seeking a job.

At other times, the team interview becomes a conversation between the two interviewers from the company, in which the interviewee is all but ignored. The interviewee leaves feeling that her time was wasted. She did not have an opportunity to sell herself, but served only as an excuse for the interviewers to chat among themselves.

The best way for interviewers to avoid these pitfalls is by choosing one person to be the lead interviewer in each team interview. That person should ask most of the questions, with the other interviewer piping in only later in the interview. Besides avoiding the pitfalls described above, having one person take the lead in the interview also permits an interviewer to follow up on a line of questions, rather than be interrupted and distracted by questions from his partner.

If the interview team consists of one person who is clearly senior to the other, make sure that the senior person is not always the lead interviewer because that will give the interviewee the sense that the junior person is being brought along only as a lackey. This impression is particularly damaging when the junior person is a woman or a member of a minority group.

Effective team interviewing also depends on both interviewers respecting one another. Remember that the interviewee will assume that the relationship demonstrated between the two interviewers is typical of the relationships between people at the company. Though there is nothing wrong with a modicum of good-natured joking between the interviewers, if the interviewee gets the impression that one of the interviewers is abusing the other, it will sour his view of the company. Be aware, too, that a joke between interviewers who know one another well may be misconstrued by the interviewee. On the other hand, a demonstration of mutual respect between the interviewers can go a long way toward making the interviewee feel that relationships between people at the company are comfortable and collegial.

I do not recommend using more than two interviewers in any job interview. It is almost impossible to create any level of comfort in the interviewee in that situation. And, for reasons discussed later in the book, I do not believe in stress interviews.

If you are being interviewed in a team situation, be prepared for interviewers who have not thought through the dynamics of conducting a successful team interview. When questions are fired at you by both interviewers, make sure that you finish answering each question. If you're interrupted, ask politely whether you may finish your answer, perhaps by saying to the second questioner, "That's a good question and I'd like to answer it, but may I first finish answering Mr. ———?"

Conversely, if you are ignored by the team interviewers, don't be bashful about inserting yourself into the conversation. Generally, just jumping in with a comment will do. You may have to do it more than once. In a particularly egregious situation, I might not be above saying, "This is an extremely interesting conversation; I'd love to participate." You have nothing to lose, since if you do not intervene, your chances of receiving an offer are extremely slim, in any case.

Finally, one suggestion may help you feel more comfortable in a team interview. Try to position yourself so you can see both interviewers without having to move your head from one side to another. This will avoid the Ping-Pong effect, and will allow you to feel and appear much more relaxed. (If you doubt this comfort factor, next time you go out with two friends, position yourself so you are forced to move your head back and forth, and notice how you feel.) If the interviewers start to position themselves so that you cannot accomplish this, you may even want to ask permission to move your chair, perhaps saying that you would find it easier if you could see and talk to both of them at once. Besides helping you to feel more comfortable, this assertiveness in positioning yourself may even serve you well in the interview because it demonstrates a certain degree of self-confidence to the interviewers.

Breaking the Rules

None of the suggestions made earlier for getting the interview off on the right foot are "rules." They are only hints as to what may help to relax both parties. Where the approaches do not seem useful or comfortable to you, don't use them. In fact, one of the most memorable interviews I ever conducted broke all of the rules as to how an interview should begin.

I was interviewing at the University of Virginia School of Law, having been on the road doing interviews at other schools for three consecutive days. My morning interviews at the law school had not been particularly successful in finding promising candidates for my firm, and the first interview of the afternoon was with a student who, though he had been a college high jump champion (having high jumped seven feet one and a half inches), was not somebody I was likely to invite back to the office. As is my practice, I noted the name of the next person I was scheduled to interview and went to the door to greet him.

In front of me stood a young man about five feet ten inches tall, wearing a conservative, blue three-piece suit, heavy horned-rimmed glasses, and wing-tipped shoes. I stuck out my hand, shook his and said, "Kaplow, tell me one thing. Can you high jump seven feet one-and-a-half inches? Because, if you can't, I'm not even interested in talking to you."

Kaplow glanced down, looked back up at me and, without skipping a beat, replied, "Not in these shoes." Kaplow became an associate at my law firm.

FOUR

THE BODY OF THE INTERVIEW:
Techniques for Making the Interview More Effective

Now that you've made it beyond the opening few minutes of the interview, what next? As we recognized in looking at the structure of the interview, the body of the interview—the evaluation, information gathering, and indirect selling stage—should consume the bulk of the interview time. In this chapter we'll explore some basic interview rules that should help both parties make the best use of the body of the interview. Then we'll focus on what specific questions to use (and avoid), and how best to answer the questions you will get.

RULES FOR THE INTERVIEWER

1. *Maintain control of the interview, but don't talk too much.* Maintaining control of the interview does not mean that you should talk most of the time; indeed, quite the opposite.

Interviewees sometimes think (wisely) that they are best off having you do most of the talking and consequently may flood you with questions. While you may emerge from that type of interview quite impressed (why? because you will have heard yourself talk and most of us are quite impressed by what we have to say), you will have learned little of value about the interviewee. You might as well stay home and base your entire decision on the resume.

A good rule of thumb is that the interviewee should be talking about 80 percent of the time in an evaluative interview, and at least 60 percent in a nonevaluative interview. Of course, all interviews are evaluative to some extent. By a nonevaluative interview, I mean one in which your focus is more on selling the interviewee than on evaluating her. Typically, this type of interview will occur after more evaluative interviews by other people at your company conclude that this is someone you probably want for the job. If you find yourself getting thirsty during interviews, you're probably talking too much.

Encourage an interviewee to talk by smiling, maintaining eye contact, nodding your head occasionally, or saying uh-huh. This will help generate open responses to your questions. If you doubt the effectiveness of this technique, watch two people at another table the next time you go to dinner. Notice how they encourage each other to talk through simple nonverbal cues.

To maintain control, follow logical lines of inquiry. Don't get sidetracked by questions posed by the interviewee. In fact, don't even permit the interviewee to ask a question for at least the first two-thirds of the interview. If the interviewee begins to ask questions early on, say, "I know you have a number of questions, and I am going to leave some time for them toward the end of the interview. But first I'd like to take some time to learn more about you, if that's okay." (In a second- or third-level interview, an interviewer should be more receptive to questions from the interviewee before the closing stage of the interview.)

If the interviewee gets off track or rambles on at great length, gently get her back by saying, "I probably was not clear enough in my question. What I really wanted to know was . . . ?" Or "That's interesting. I wish we had more time to discuss it, but I'd like to move on to . . ." Of course, an interviewee who persists in not answering questions, rambling on, or asking questions is revealing something about herself.

On the other hand, do not cut off interviewees' responses too quickly, or finish their sentences for them. Besides being rude, that will curtail the amount of information you will get. Interviewees should also be careful not to interrupt interviewers. Refusing to let an interviewer complete his thought is not a sign of commendable aggressiveness or motivation. It is rude and arrogant. If you do it, your chances of getting an offer will be slim.

2. *Listen.* Listening is hard work. It involves much more than not talking, or simply hearing. It is an active endeavor that demands that you be awake and alert, concentrate totally on what is being said, and clear your mind of other concerns.

To listen effectively you must be nonjudgmental. Do not react to negative information. If, when an interviewee tells you something you regard as negative, you fall off your chair or blurt out "You've got to be kidding," that is the last piece of negative information you will get. Play down bad news by indicating that it's not an uncommon experience (if that is true) or just by listening and encouraging elaboration of the news.

Try to understand the interviewee *as he sees himself.* Many answers are susceptible to more than one interpretation so it is important not to jump to conclusions. For example, suppose an interviewee tells you, "I prefer the opportunity to work at my own pace." You may think this means (a) he is slow and does not like to be pushed, (b) he is fast and does not like to be reigned in, (c) he does not work well under pressure, (d) he is a self-starter, or (e) he does not take supervision well. Unless you listen, ask the interviewee to explain his answer, and then explore specific situations in which the interviewee has worked at his own pace (or has not been able to do so), you cannot know what he means.

Ask the interviewee to spell out carefully what he means and to repeat answers if there is any ambiguity or uncertainty. Don't be afraid to say, "I'd like you to slow down just a bit. Could you please go back to . . . ?" or "I'm not sure I understood that last sequence. Could you walk me through it again?"

You can hear things much more quickly than they can be spoken, so you must find a way to utilize your excess time. Try the following techniques as ways of getting yourself to listen:

- Imagine where the discussion is leading.
- Weigh the evidence you are receiving.
- Review what's been said so far.
- Summarize the point the speaker is trying to make.
- Ask yourself whether what you are hearing is helpful.
- Look for ways to use the information the speaker is giving.
- Decide whether what is being said makes sense.
- Check whether you seem to be getting the whole story.
- Determine whether the points being made are backed up with examples.
- Compare how what you are hearing relates to what you already know.
- Assess what biases may be blocking your listening.

Listen between the lines—note the interviewee's non-verbal communication such as gestures, tone of voice, and facial expressions. Is she extremely nervous, or self-possessed? Is she somebody in whom others are likely to have confidence? As Yogi Berra once said, "You can observe a lot just by watching." (Beware, though, that these observations may lead you to jump to conclusions too quickly.) Do not become so preoccupied with observing and thinking ahead, though, that you are not listening to what the interviewee is saying.

It may seem strange to say so, but real listening takes courage. You may emerge from the interview changed; you may prove yourself wrong.

3. *Show you are listening by using an interviewee's responses in your questions, commenting after the question and following up.* Assume you ask an interviewee, "What aspects of your last job did you find rewarding?" and she responds that she enjoyed working with the other people on the team. Instead of dropping the line of questioning there, probe further by asking, "What was it about working with other people that you enjoyed?", or, "Can you tell me about a situation in which you particularly enjoyed working on a team?" Alternatively, you may explore the opposite of the answer by asking, "What difficulties did you find in working on a project with a team of people?" Using the candidate's answer in your next question will automatically result in follow-up.

You might preface your next question with a comment such as, "Yes, I find that working as a team with my cohorts is one of the most enjoyable aspects of my work, too. What was it about working with the people that you enjoyed?" This type of comment accomplishes three purposes: (a) it makes the interview more conversational, (b) it helps to establish rapport with interviewee, and (c) it subtly sells your company by alluding to your own teamwork.

The same technique is useful for the interviewee. If you can take something the interviewer has said and relate it to your own experience, abilities, or desires, you not only will have shown that you are listening to the interviewer, but you will also have helped to establish rapport with him.

4. *Don't form even a preliminary decision as to whether you are going to make an offer for at least twenty minutes.* Some interviewees take awhile to get going. Delaying your decision will allow you to give the slow-starting interviewee a fair opportunity to prove himself. It will also keep you interested in the interview because once you've ruled a candidate out it's hard to continue to listen.

Withholding judgment helps you avoid mistakes on the other side of the ledger, too. Certain interviewees who make a favorable initial impression (often because of their resume) demonstrate, when given half a chance, that they are not worthy of receiving an offer.

By allowing the interviewee to talk before you decide, you give him a chance to emerge as a person, instead of prejudging him based on an item or two on his resume. During the interview, you should be forming and exploring hypotheses about the interviewee. When you are able to corroborate a hypothesis you have formed in more than one setting, you will begin to get more comfortable with your evaluation.

5. *Use past behavior to predict future behavior.* The way a person acted in the past is the best guide to how he will act in the future. The past experiences you explore do not have to be related to the present position. As we will see in the next two chapters, you can learn a lot about how a person will perform in your company by discussing parts of the interviewee's background that may seem remote.

Too many interviewers cover a significant job experience with a brief question or two, then move on. Here are thirteen questions you can ask about almost any job:

1. How did you get the job?
2. What were your expectations about the job?
3. In what ways were those expectations met, disappointed, or exceeded?
4. What were your responsibilities?
5. What did you like/find satisfying about the job?
6. Why did you like that?
7. What did you dislike/find frustrating about the job?
8. Why did you dislike that/how did you deal with the frustration?
9. Did you run into any difficult or stressful situations?
10. How did you deal with those situations?
11. How would you describe the people who supervised you?
12. What did you learn from the job that will stay with you?
13. If you had to do it over again, what would you do differently in that job experience?

My point is not that you should ask these questions of every interviewee, but that you should have them in your repertoire for use, when appropriate. Of course, an interviewee's answers to these questions probably will suggest other follow-up questions.

Elicit specific situations to illuminate the interviewee's responses. Do not be content with statements about what an interviewee would "usually," "typically," or "generally" do. For example, if the interviewee says he did not generally like having to go through many drafts of a document, ask for a specific instance in which that occurred, then ask what the interviewee actually did, said, felt, and/or thought at the time. Similarly, if the interviewee liked the opportunity to complete a project on her own, ask for an example of such a project, then find out what the interviewee did, said, felt, and/or thought.

Interviewees often need to be prompted to give you the information you are seeking. Tell the interviewee you are looking for a rather detailed description of what he did in a situation so you can be sure you understand what was involved. When he provides a level of detail you are looking for, encourage him to continue to provide that detail by saying, "Thanks, that's the type of description that's helpful to me. Can you think of another example of . . . ?" The idea is to keep the interviewee talking in the past tense about a specific experience or situation. You want to learn what the person did at the time, rather than his current reflections on the situation. While those current thoughts may suggest a person's flexibility and capacity to learn from experience, the thoughts become significant only if they affect the interviewee's behavior.

The same method, probing deeply by asking many different questions, holds true if you are exploring a specific characteristic of a candidate. For example, if you were trying to determine whether she could persuade others to her position, you might pursue the following line of questions: Can you tell me about a time when you had to convince another person to adopt your position on a matter? Who was the other person? What was your position? What was the other person's position? What led up to the situation? What strategy did you adopt? What objections did the other person raise? What did you think was the other person's real, principal concern? How did you deal with the other person's objections and concerns? What did you say? What did the other person say? How much did you talk? What was the outcome? What is your current relationship with the other person? What, if anything, might you do differently if you encountered a similar situation today? Can you give me an example of a time when you acted differently?

In exploring what an interviewee did in the past, make sure you distinguish between a situation in which the person had no real responsibility and one in which she had a significant role. Get the person to describe precisely what her role was by asking, "What did you do?" The better she can describe it, the more likely she did it. Do not be content with a description by an interviewee of what *"we"* did; ask what *"she"* did.

Make sure you understand exactly who the players were in the situation she describes. Being assertive toward a supervisor shows quite a different quality than being assertive toward a colleague or subordinate.

An interviewee should be prepared to answer all of the above questions about any job she has had (or characteristic she possesses). Review these questions prior to an interview because they may suggest areas you may wish to discuss in response to a more general question such as, "Tell me about your job." Imagine what follow-up questions an astute interviewer might ask, and think about how you might respond. Also, remember that when you are seeking information from an interviewer, you should use the same approach outlined above to get detailed, specific information.

6. *Use silence, both after a question and at the end of an answer.* Here's a rule of thumb you should apply: When you ask a question, don't be the next person to talk. A certain amount of time is appropriate for an interviewee to think about an answer. If the interviewee says nothing for half an hour, you will have learned quite a bit about her suitability for the job.

After an interviewee appears to have completed his answer, wait a few seconds before asking another question. During these few seconds, the interviewee may be deciding whether to add something to his answer. Your silence implies that you expect (or will welcome) more. Some interviewees will retract what they have said, or modify their answers. Others will provide more information. Often something that is added by an interviewee during these few seconds of silence can prove more revealing than the initial answer.

Silence is uncomfortable. You will feel pressure internally to keep the flow of the interview going by speaking. (Indeed, this pressure is one of the things that leads to interviewers talking too much.) But if you learn to resist that pressure, you will receive better information.

Of course, silence is also uncomfortable for an interviewee. As interviewee, though, you should not hesitate to take the time you need to formulate an answer. When you are confronted with silence at the end of your answer, don't feel obligated to add to what you've said. Certainly you should not modify or retract your answer because of the silence. Frequently, the silence merely reflects an interviewer trying to formulate his next question. Where the silence drags on, you have several choices: (a) remain silent and await the next question, (b) ask the interviewer whether you have answered his question, (c) suggest another question for the interviewer by saying, "Perhaps you'd like to hear about . . . ?," or, (d) ask the interviewer a question. Any of these approaches is acceptable.

7. *Don't use stress (unnecessarily).* Direct, stressful questions may test a candidate's interviewing skill, but it won't test his job skills. The way a person reacts to stress in an interview is not a good indicator of how he will react on the job. The interview gives the interviewer an unfair advantage and creates an artificial situation that will not apply in business. Interview stress derives from an interviewee's belief that getting the job depends on a single, irreversible, time-limited performance. Job pressure is more sustained, with repeated opportunities to perform. Furthermore, stress produces a protective reaction in an interviewee that means you will get both less candid and less complete responses to your other questions.

Stress interviews will not help you hire candidates you want. Put bluntly, torture doesn't sell. As an interviewer it's easy to abuse interviewees, and they are generally not impressed by it. Interviewees see interviewers who use stress as arrogant. Stress questions, which will be discussed again in the chapter entitled "The Worst Questions Employers Ask," are regarded by interviewees as blatant evidence that the interviewer considers the interview a game.

Properly phrased questions may produce a certain amount of stress by forcing an interviewee to think about himself and his experience. This type of stress, however, is an inevitable by-product of probing for information that will be valuable in making your hiring decision. Likewise, in some instances, you may stimulate stress as you ask for specific information that you need to make your decision, such as questions about a candidate's performance in a previous job or information about a period of time that is not accounted for by the resume.

As an interviewee, if you are confronted by interviewers who feel that stress is an effective interview technique, don't fall into the trap of getting angry, combative, or flustered. A simple smile at the interviewer will let her know you are aware of what is going on. You may then respond with something like, "That's an interesting/unusual question. Let me think about it for a minute (then take time to formulate your answer)." Another approach would be to say, "That's an interesting/unusual question. May I ask why are you interested in my answer to that question?"

8. *Don't shy away from asking questions you need to ask just because they may be uncomfortable.* For example, if information about a candidate's academic performance is important, ask about it. Interviewees expect those questions, anyway. Questions about sensitive matters are best asked in the middle of the interview—after you've established rapport

with the interviewee; but not at the end, because you don't want to close the interview on an uncomfortable topic.

Make sure you get all the factual information you will need. Too often, interviewers complete an interview and find they don't have the information necessary to make a decision. This results in either (a) the embarrassment of having to go back to the interviewee to get the information, (b) the foolishness of rejecting somebody who might be a good candidate, or (c) the wasted time caused by inviting somebody in for further interviews and then rejecting him based on information that was available before he came in.

Though you should not avoid asking tough questions, you may be able to soften their impact by using introductory phrases. For example, phrases such as "Do you imagine that," "Do you think that," "I wonder whether," "May it be, perhaps, that," "Is it possible that," "Do you suppose that," and "Do you believe that" can help to make some difficult questions less threatening to the interviewee.

9. *Take notes during the interview.* Particularly in an on-campus interview, it is difficult to remember what an interviewee says if you do not take notes. Also, something said early in the interview that you did not pay much attention to may prove significant later on.

Some interviewees may find note taking uncomfortable. But if you mention at the outset that you are intending to take notes, explain the reason why and ask the interviewee's permission, interviewees will not object. For example, you may say, "I'm going to be speaking to a number of candidates for this position [today] and I'd like to be able to remember what we've talked about, so, if you don't mind, I'd like to take some notes."

If you take notes, do so steadily during the interview, not only when an interviewee says something negative. Your notes should be sufficiently complete and legible to allow you to discuss the basis for your conclusions with a colleague after the interview. While taking notes, hold the pad upright so the candidate cannot read what you are writing. And be careful about which matters you choose to write down. Though a note on a particular physical or personal characteristic of the interviewee may help you to remember her, it may also prove an embarrassing piece of evidence against you in a discriminatory hiring claim.

Some interviewers are not comfortable taking notes during the interview and prefer to make brief notes after the interview, or to dictate something quickly into a tape recorder. Obviously, if you are not comfortable taking notes, you should not do so. As soon as you can after the interview, though, jot down or expand on any notes you have taken. Also, if you are in a situation in which you will be seeing many candidates in a row, begin to make preliminary decisions on each candidate as you go along.

Interviewees should not be offended if an interviewer takes notes, even if he is somewhat awkward at doing it. Instead, regard note taking as an indication that the interviewer is taking the interview seriously.

10. *Assume you are interested in hiring each interviewee to whom you speak.* If you find that difficult to believe five minutes into the interview, remember that, almost invariably, the person you have the least interest in during an interview season will be the best friend of the person you are most interested in hiring. (I've found this best friend syndrome to be almost statistically provable.) Showing disinterest in the "dud" may kill your chances of hiring the "star." And, besides, some duds five minutes into an interview turn out to be attractive candidates twenty-five minutes later. Not many, perhaps, but some.

Show interest in each interviewee as a person; approach each interview determined to learn something new from the interviewee. (The same, of course, holds true for the interviewee. Just as you like to find an interviewer who is interested in you as a human being, the interviewer also will appreciate your interest in him as a person.) Even the least interesting interviewees are not as dull as you may think if you give them a chance to talk about something that *they* are interested in. To be sure, that is not always true. Some interviewees (as well as some interviewers) *are* dull. They will give you a whole new appreciation for the length of half an hour, reminding you that it is composed of thirty individual minutes, each of which itself contains sixty quite separate and distinct seconds.

Of course, if you are conducting a so-called "courtesy interview" in which you talk to a candidate solely because he is a friend or relative of somebody at your company or one of your customers, it will be difficult to assume you are interested in hiring the interviewee (because you are not). Courtesy interviews are neither courtesies nor interviews. They are games. Avoid them whenever possible, and when you cannot avoid them, try to set them up as sessions in which you are advising the person you are speaking to, rather than pretending you are conducting a job interview.

Interviewees who are granted interviews through connections with family or friends should be aware that these may be "courtesy" interviews. If you value your time and do not care to participate in a charade, have your friend or family member ask whether you are regarded as a serious candidate. Confronted with this type of direct question, most companies will answer honestly.

You may cling to the illusion that even in a courtesy interview, you will emerge as the winning candidate. But an interviewer who conducts a courtesy interview has created a self-fulfilling prophecy. Worse than an interviewer who makes up her mind in the first five minutes of an interview, the courtesy interviewer has made up her mind before the interview even begins. If you want to get information through a meeting (not an interview) set up by a friend or family member, by all means do so. But don't kid yourself into thinking a courtesy interview is a real interview.

RULES FOR THE INTERVIEWEE

1. *Be yourself; relax.* Too many interviewees try to be the person they think the interviewer wants to hire. Usually, that fails. You've been playing yourself for so long it's hard to switch.

Playing another role may not be such a good idea, in any case. You may be wrong about what you think the interviewer wants. But even if you correctly assessed who the interviewer wanted, and even if you were successful in playing that role, it would still be a bad idea. Once you got on the job, you would be unhappy because you cannot play a role forever.

Of course, you *do* need to do more in an interview than simply be yourself. I am reminded of a wonderful *New Yorker* cartoon in which a person sitting across the desk from an interviewee asks, "Any qualifications other than being very comfortable with yourself?"

Being yourself will help you to relax; playing a role makes you tense. As suggested in "Preparing for the Interview: Interviewee," being well prepared and keeping the interview process in perspective—recognizing that not receiving an offer is not the worst thing in the world, that some rejection is inevitable and that the interview process is an imperfect science—should also help you to relax.

2. *Don't feel you have to agree with everything the interviewer says, or be a sycophant, bowing and scraping in homage.* Though interviewers, being human, may appreciate a little flattery, some interviewees carry this to excess. Just as outstanding interviewees are wary of interviewers who fawn

over them, interviewers believe that candidates who think their company is perfect may not be so darn good themselves.

Most interviewers recognize that they need somebody who has the ability to stand up for himself, to disagree when appropriate, to show some self-confidence. A sycophantic interviewee will be thought not to possess those important characteristics. Indeed, some interviewers may even say things they don't agree with to test your assertiveness and self-confidence.

When you do disagree with an interviewer, though, do so respectfully. Instead of laughing and saying, "That's the most idiotic thing I ever heard in my life," try saying "that's a good point, but . . ." or "that's one way of looking at it, but I tend to see it this way . . ." On the other hand, if it really *is* the most idiotic thing you ever heard in your life, maybe you shouldn't resist saying so. After all, there *are* other jobs, and do you want to work for that idiot, anyway?

3. *Make a bad interviewer into a good interviewer.* Don't assume that the interviewer is an expert at what he's doing. Typically, he doesn't know much about interviewing at all. His "real work" is something else. (That is the way many interviewers, pretending to be joking, distinguish between what they get paid for and their interviewing responsibilities.) A good interviewee, though, can make an interviewer look good, no matter how poor an interview the interviewer is conducting. By applying the techniques described in this book, you can make the interview go well for the interviewer—and thus for yourself—even with someone who's not a very good interviewer.

4. *Acknowledge your mistakes.* If you have said something incorrect during the interview and later realize it, don't be afraid to correct yourself. If a question by an interviewer calls for discussing a situation in which you made a mistake in a job, or in school, admit it. In a sense, your willingness to

acknowledge mistakes is a strength because it demonstrates both humility and self-confidence.

You may even be able to show your sense of humor in admitting a mistake, as this candidate did in his preinterview letter to a prominent San Francisco law firm:

> Dear Ms.————:
>
> I recently wrote to you expressing an interest in permanent employment at _____. I would like to inform you that I will be in the San Francisco area in November and would appreciate the opportunity to set up an interview.
>
> In my cover letter, I indicated to you that I was a first-year law student. After further review I have discovered that I am a third-year law student. I apologize for the confusion.
>
> Once again, thank you for your consideration. I look forward to hearing from you.
>
> Sincerely,

5. *Recognize and respect the fine, but important, line between self-confidence and arrogance.* If you cross over that line, you are going to turn what may be one of your strongest selling points into a fatal flaw.

Often, the difference is not so much in what is said, but in *how* it is said. Compare, for example, the following two answers to the question, "Do you think you could handle making a presentation to a senior corporate officer?"

"Yes, I'm quite confident I could handle that. In my prior position with X corporation, I presented a proposal to the chief executive officer of the company, Mr. Nesbit, that we reorganize the way we were handling our business travel. We spent about an hour and a half together discussing my proposal and eventually he accepted it, with a few small modifications."

"Oh sure, that would be absolutely no problem for me. I used to do that all the time over at X corporation. I remember the time old Bob Nesbit, the CEO, asked me to noodle over what we were doing with business travel. Bob just flipped over the solution I came up with."

An interviewer is sometimes more interested in how you answer a question than in the substance of your answer.

Do not drop names. By that I mean both dropping the last name, that is referring to important people by their first name, as in the second example above; and using the name of a well-known person you know, just for effect. Name dropping signals to an interviewer a certain arrogance and need to impress. Of course, you may mention the names of important people with whom you have worked in a context that fits appropriately into the interview discussion.

6. *Beware of the perfect company.* It doesn't exist. If you are getting the impression that the company you are talking to has no flaws, either you're not digging deep enough, or the people with whom you are speaking are not being candid. Use the questioning techniques suggested earlier for interviewers to get at the information you want.

7. *Talk to people at the level at which you will be working in the company.* These employees' experiences will most likely mirror what you will find at the company, and they are more likely to be candid with you than will more senior employees who may have swallowed, or even invented, the company line. It's not necessarily that senior people will *lie* to you. They may simply not know what it is like to work at your level.

8. *Be sensible about how you dress and groom yourself.* Many interview books spend pages and pages advising interviewees on what to wear, purporting to give absolute rules, including one that advises "Never wear a brown suit." Hogwash. If you have a brown suit you like, wear it.

Other books advise interviewees always to carry a briefcase. If you feel comfortable with a briefcase—or need it for physical or emotional balance—carry it. If not, don't.

The real rule for how to dress and what to carry is to use common sense. Look neat and clean. Don't smell, either from body odor or excessive commercial odor. Dress appropriately for the position for which you are applying. Don't wear jewelry that is going to jangle or distract. Don't smoke or chew gum. Don't carry two briefcases. Comb your hair, if you have any (don't be like the balding candidate who reportedly excused himself from an interview and returned to the office a few minutes later wearing a hairpiece). Polish your shoes. Do not slouch in the chair. (One friend reported to me that in an interview with a senior officer he had a kind of out-of-body experience in which it seemed that the interviewer was getting taller and taller. Finally, my friend realized that he'd slipped down in his chair, practically sliding off. Turned out he had the flu.) You'll be able to add to this list, if you just *think* about how you would react to somebody, if you were the interviewer. Dressing inappropriately is a form of showing disrespect for the interviewer.

Don't try to trick people with your dress. The story goes that a first-year law student at Stanford showed up for an interview in tennis attire. He apologized profusely for his attire and explained that the recruiting office had screwed up and just moments before the interview notified him of the interview. He did not receive an offer. He interviewed in tennis attire with the same person at the same firm the next year and told the same story. He did not receive an offer, again.

Your failure to use common sense in the area of dress is likely to have two effects, neither of which will help you get a job. First, it may make the interviewer uncomfortable. Second, and more important, it will mark you as lacking in good judgment, a trait that most every employer seeks in most every employee.

On the other hand, don't dress in a way that makes you uncomfortable. If you always wear a bow tie, wear a bow tie. If you never wear high heels, don't wear high heels. I can't assure you that those decisions will not mean that some employer will decide not to make you an offer. But do you really want to work for that employer, anyway?

9. *Do not go out of your way to criticize other employers with whom you have worked or are interviewing.* Most interviewers regard this as showing poor taste, and poor judgment. Even worse than bad-mouthing your prior employer is revealing confidential information learned in the course of your employment. That will brand you as untrustworthy and doom your candidacy.

If you are asked a question and an honest answer requires some criticism of another employer, do so in a measured, specific, and respectful manner. Thus, for example, if you are asked what you thought of the training you received from another employer, you might say, "I think the feedback on projects could have been more prompt and complete," rather than, "It was awful, I couldn't wait to get the hell out of there."

10. *Don't be afraid to show your enthusiasm for anything, even a job you may regard as rather menial.* Similarly, no matter how many times you may have been asked a particular question, avoid sounding bored or appearing to give a pat answer. Though you may have given the answer twenty-five times, this is the first and only time this interviewer will have heard it.

Finally, do not take advice given by interview books (even this one) as gospel. Nobody has a corner on wisdom in the interview. In this book, I've scattered a few examples of advice given by other so-called experts that I did not consider wise. I'm sure others could do the same with some examples from this book. Interviewees should exercise some judgment about which expert advice to follow. And you should exercise the same degree of discretion in determining whether to follow the advice you receive from placement directors, friends, and relatives.

FIVE

USING RESUME EXCERPTS TO LEARN ABOUT A CANDIDATE

You've already spent considerable time and effort determining what you're looking for in a candidate. And in the preceding chapter we took a look at some basic techniques that will help you get at that information. In this chapter we'll focus on how to use candidates' resumes, which constitute the raw material for shaping the interview.

Appropriately enough, the resume presents the best side of the interviewee; you'll almost never see anything negative. Interviewees are coached to make their experience sound lofty on the resume. Sometimes they make it appear as if they ran the company during their position last summer. Don't judge candidates too harshly for doing this. You would do the same thing. This tendency of candidates to gild the lily, though, is one reason it is important to use the interview to probe the candidate's actual experiences so you can get information on his weaknesses, as well as his strengths.

Of course, as an interviewer you are not limited to what

is on the resume. And you will definitely want to dig far deeper than the material presented there. To do that you must become adept at analyzing the information on the resume, and figuring out how you might use that information as the skeleton to build a model of the candidate.

To that end, consider the excerpts below, taken from actual resumes submitted to employers, modified only slightly to change dates and personal references. I invite you to go through each of these resume items, asking yourself the following questions:

1. If this appeared on the resume of a candidate you were interviewing, would you be likely to ask about it?
2. Why are you deciding to ask or not to ask about this item?
3. If you were to ask about this topic, what might you learn about the candidate?
4. What assumptions may you be making about the candidate based on this resume item?

By analyzing these excerpts, you will begin to develop your strategy for conducting the interview. You will force yourself to consider not only what elements of a resume you would ask about, but *why* you might ask about them and what that information might lead to. You will become more aware of the assumptions you may be making on the basis of a resume item, and of the need to challenge your assumptions. Interviewees will understand from this exercise how and why an interviewer may choose to explore a wide range of topics from a resume. That knowledge should help you both in constructing your resume and in preparing for the interview.

In comments below each of these excerpts, I have given you my personal reaction to them. My reaction is not necessarily the "correct" one, only one you may find interesting to compare to your own reaction.

Note that I make a lot of assumptions about what I may learn from these excerpts. Undoubtedly some, perhaps many, of my assumptions will be wrong. Recognize that you will be wrong in some of the assumptions you make, too. For example, if you see that a candidate is editor of *The Gazette*, her college newspaper, do you assume that she is popular with her peers, a good leader, deals effectively with stress, and writes well? You might be right. But, on exploration, you may find the person was chosen by a faculty member, that nobody else wanted the position, and that she is a prima donna who is primarily interested in the title. Part of the joy of interviewing is the surprises, the opportunities to prove yourself wrong.

1. Article entitled, "Digital Audio Tape Systems: The Current Challenge to the American Copyright System," *Copyright Industries Journal* (April, 1993).

   COMMENT: I'd think this person has technical expertise. I do not, so my natural tendency might be to steer clear of this topic. I would be likely to ask about it, though, because I would want to determine whether this person could explain the article in a way that was understandable to me.

2. MCI Telecomunications, Inc.,   Commercial Sales
   Boston, MA   Representative
       Sold long-distance telephone services to small
       businesses in New York and New England.
       Managed all aspects of sale, from cold call to
       equipment installation and customer satisfaction.

   COMMENT: This person has experienced a lot of rejection. I would want to find out how he dealt with it, and learn what elements of the job he liked or disliked, and why. I would expect to learn quite a bit about the interviewee's ability to deal with adversity and to relate to a customer from this discussion. Note that the interviewee has misspelled "Tele-communications." I regard this as a potentially significant—though not fatal—error. I'd explore the degree of care the interviewee brings to his work. (Interviewees beware: Proof-read your resume *carefully*. If you have one page in which to present yourself, that page ought to be perfect.)

3. Joyce Beverages, Inc., New Rochelle, NY
Plant Line Operator Summers 1987–1989
> Operated material-handling equipment and
> mechanized-beverage-bottling- and canning-line
> machinery.

COMMENT: This person dealt with repetitive, routine tasks. I'd want to know how she handled this, how she related to others on the job. Note that this is a position the person held for three summers. I'd like to know what progress, if any, she made during that time. Has she thought about this experi-ence, and how it may help her in another position?

4. Trends Management Talent Agency   Academic Year
London, England   1990–91
> Danced with a professional dance company in
> theaters, nightclubs, and casinos throughout
> London, and for the British Broadcasting Company.

COMMENT: My instinct is to assume that this is the resume of a woman. Obviously, this would be a fun experience to talk about. It might be a good icebreaker to open with. How-ever, this item strikes me as such a "grabber" that it would be discussed by every interviewer. That would make me less inclined to spend time on it (depending upon what else was on the resume). I try to avoid talking about the same things other interviewers discuss because I find interviewees develop pat responses to those topics. If I did ask about this experience, I'd try to find a twist the interviewee might not have encoun-tered before. For example, I might ask the person to compare the experience dancing in a theater with that of dancing in a nightclub.

5. Interests: lap swimming, racquetball, outdoor sports, and contemporary art

COMMENT: I am a lap swimmer so I might well start the interview by talking a bit about that. The other items listed could also serve as icebreakers.

6. WIP-610 AM Metromedia Radio,
Philadelphia   (Sept.–Dec. '90)
Reporter, covered home Sixers, Flyers, and Phillies games. Responsible for conducting locker-room interviews and writing copy to be aired.

COMMENT: As a sports fan, I would love to talk about this. I have a little of the same reaction to this as I do to the professional dancing "grabber," however. Again, if I did discuss this, I would think of an angle other interviewers might not have used. For example, I might ask how the candidate reacted to having his copy revised, or what he thought of the way the on-the-air people performed what he had written.

7. Cotranslation of Book: *Handbuch der Weltpolitischen Analyse,* (by Daniel Frei and Dieter Ruloff) from the German, 1988

COMMENT: I would be fascinated to learn the intricacies and difficulties involved in translation. Note that this is a cotranslation, so I would want to know about the relationship between the candidate and his cotranslator. This seems to me an interesting aspect of the job because I would expect that a lot of quite personal choices go into translating. That would mean the person would have to negotiate a lot with his cotranslator and come to agreements on what might be some rather emotional issues. I would also want to hear how well the person explains what is involved in translating, and how he came to undertake this particular project.

8. Self-Employed Auctioneer   1985–Present
Auction merchandise in satisfaction of garage and storage liens.

COMMENT: This person may well be quite an entrepreneur. I would like to know how she got into the business. I would also be interested in knowing the problems involved in being a good auctioneer, and how this person dealt with them.

9. "Beyond the Factory Walls: Female Factory Workers and the Industrialization of Taiwan, 1950–1985," April 1990. Senior thesis.

COMMENT: Though I am not particularly interested in the subject matter, I almost always ask about a candidate's senior thesis. I am interested in knowing whether he can explain it succinctly and understandably. If a candidate pleads that it's been too long ago for him to remember, I regard it as poor judgment to have listed the thesis on the resume.
By way of contrast, I almost never asked law students about law review articles they had written. I found students almost always had a pat description virtually committed to memory. In fact, I came to regard dissection of a person's law review article in an interview as akin to discussing a bodily ailment at a dinner party. I try to avoid both.

10. *PLANNING BOARD MEMBER*
Voorhees Township Planning Board, Voorhees, New Jersey
    Acted on applications that involved subdivisions, site
    plans, and conditional uses. Worked with
    engineers, attorneys, planners, and developers.
    Updated Township Master Plan. Very active in
    the community.

COMMENT: This person has worked with a lot of different kinds of people in situations that may well become emotionally charged. I would want to know how she dealt with that. I'd also like to know how she got the position. For example, if it were an elected post, that might suggest a whole range of characteristics the person might possess, such as willingness to get into the fray, toughness, comfort in communicating to large groups, etc.

11. TRIBUNAL ADMINISTRATOR
American Arbitration Association—New York City, NY
Prepared and supervised administrative details of arbitration cases from initiation to final disposition, attended hearings to assist arbitrators and parties and to ensure compliance with procedural and statutory standards.

COMMENT: I don't have a good idea what this person *did*, from the description. Was this a routine job, or one that involved some real initiative and creativity? What does "supervised" mean? Whom did he supervise, and how? I would probably explore this job experience in detail to try to learn that. Even if it were routine, though, I might learn quite a lot about the person by asking how he dealt with the required tasks.

12. Special Olympics Coach,   1985–1987
Santa Barbara, CA

COMMENT: My assumption is that this is a caring, kind person. I would want to know what got him involved in coaching, what satisfactions and disappointments he experienced, and how he dealt with them. I might also ask what caused him to stop coaching.

13. Carpenter, Austin, Texas   6/89–8/90

COMMENT: Having absolutely no carpentry skills (other than being a whiz at using cellophane tape), I'd like to know all about this candidate's carpentry experience. Was he on his own? How did he generate work? What types of projects did he undertake? How interested was he in the artistry involved? In seeing that the job was done perfectly? Did he do this part-time, while in school (Austin is a college town)? If so, how did he balance the work with his school responsibilities?

14. CENTURY 21, RAND ASSOCIATES, 1987–1988
New York City, NY
Licensed real estate salesperson: Involved in the listing and sale of residential homes.

COMMENT: I would explore this job experience to find out whether the candidate really related to his clients, or whether he saw it purely as a way to make some money. What qualities did it take to succeed in getting listings? In making sales? Why did he hold the job for only a year or two?

15. UNIVERSITY OF 2/88–2/89
CALIFORNIA,
SAN FRANCISCO
Puppet Therapist
Created and performed preoperative puppet shows
for pediatric patients and their parents to
familiarize them with hospital procedures.

COMMENT: This sounds like a fascinating job. Even though it's a "grabber" that most every interviewer would talk about, I could not resist discussing it. To avoid getting pat responses from the interviewee, I would try to probe one or two experiences she had in the position in depth.

16. UNITED PARCEL SERVICE SUMMER 1987
Uniondale, New York
Customer Relations Liaison: Expedited the retrieval
of misplaced packages, coordinated delivery, and
established shipping schedules.

COMMENT: This is somebody who has operated under fire. I'd like to know how she dealt with it. Did she develop empathy for the angry customers she encountered, or regard them as royal pains? Does she have any ideas for making the service more effective, or did she deal narrowly with her job?

17. National Accordion Champion, 1989
State Accordion Champion, New York 1984–1988.

COMMENT: I envision Lawrence Welk saying, "A-wunnerful, a-wunnerful." I'd like to know what goes into being a champion accordion player, how the person chose that instrument, and whether the pressures are akin to pressures felt by championship athletes. I'd be interested in whether accordion playing is a growing or dwindling art form. I'd also try to learn something about the history of the accordion and whether anyone well-known composed for it. I'd hope to find something to slip into a conversation at my next cocktail party.

18. LYCEE AL MATAR, Nador, Morocco   9/85–7/87
Teacher, U.S. Peace Corps

COMMENT: I envision a liberal, do-good, adventurous type. Obviously, the intercultural experience would be interesting to explore with this candidate. I'd try to do that with specificity. For example, what differences in Moroccan society did you personally find it difficult to adjust to? Why? How did you deal with those difficulties?

19. Summer 1988
Cofounded the FASA Corporation, a game design and manufacturing company, Chicago, IL. Set up office, manufacturing, and distribution operations.

COMMENT: Appears to be an entrepreneur. I'd be interested in whether the project succeeded or failed, what problems she encountered and how she dealt with them, what were the relations with the cofounder and whether the company is still operating. I would also like to know what kind of games the company manufactured.

20. MEYER'S MESSENGER SERVICE   6/88–6/90
New York, New York

Full-time and part-time bicycle messenger.

COMMENT: This person is a daredevil. I would like to know what's involved in being a successful bicycle messenger, what interesting experiences he encountered and whether he killed anybody in the process.

As you can see from my comments, I might explore any of these twenty resume excerpts—most of them at considerable length—in an interview. In general, any item on a resume may provide fertile ground for exploration in an interview. Of course, probing an interviewee's experiences is not always without risk. One of my former partners once encountered a candidate who had served in the CIA for several years. My partner said, "I guess I can't ask too much about your CIA experience because you couldn't talk about it." The interviewee replied, "Oh, no, you can feel free to ask. And I could tell you about it—but, I'd have to kill you afterward." My partner is still living.

The CIA to the contrary, I am always interested in exploring any prior-job experiences because those hold the most promising clues to discovering how an interviewee will perform in the position for which I am interviewing. For those who may not be familiar with it, I recommend a book called *Working* by Studs Terkel, which consists of interviews Terkel conducted with people who hold widely varying jobs, from elevator operator to doctor. Through his expert interviewing ability, Terkel gets working people to talk openly about their feelings about their jobs and, in the process, makes his readers appreciate the depth and dignity possible in any line of work—and how much you can learn about a person from discussing any job experience.

SIX

DECIDING WHAT QUESTIONS TO ASK

We've looked at resume excerpts to identify what areas you might explore in an interview, and why. Now it's time to analyze a range of questions to determine whether they will help gather the information you need.

Types of questions

Before we look at specific questions, though, let's consider seven categories of questions, and whether they may prove useful:

1. *Open-ended* Questions that begin with "how," "why," and "what" invite an interviewee to answer at length, cause the interview to flow as a conversation, and permit the interviewee to do most of the talking.
2. *Closed-ended* These questions can be answered "yes" or "no," and begin with words such as "did,"

"have," "do," "would," and "are." Because they do not encourage the interviewee to talk, these questions will put pressure on you to keep the interview going by asking another question. Instead of listening to the interviewee, you are likely to be thinking about what your next question will be. Interviewers who report trouble getting interviewees to talk sometimes play a role in their problem by asking too many closed-ended questions. (Of course, closed-ended questions are effective when you are seeking specific information.)

Practice converting closed-ended questions to open-ended questions. For example, instead of "Did you like your job last summer?" say "Tell me about your job last summer." or ask "What did you enjoy about your job last summer?" Instead of asking, "Are you a team player?" try "Tell me about a situation in which you worked or participated as a member of a team." And instead of saying, "Are you a hard worker?" ask the interviewee, "Tell me about a typical day for you."

An interviewee, of course, may go beyond a one-word response, even when the interviewer does ask a closed-ended question. An interviewer who asks, "Did you enjoy your job last summer?" wants to know not only *whether* you enjoyed it, but *why* you did or did not enjoy it. Answering with one word will produce the type of awkward silence that increases the tension level in interviews. (On the other hand, don't babble on interminably. Once you've answered the question, stop.) Of course, when the interviewer clearly is seeking specific information, such as, "Did you hold that job before you went to graduate school?" It is perfectly appropriate to answer with a simple "Yes" or "No, just after."

3. *Leading*   These questions lead an interviewee to the answer you want and should be avoided. For example, "Would you say you have the analytical ability for this job?" or "Would you be interested in working for a company that is as large as ours?" Who would expect an interviewee to answer "no" to either of those questions? Remember that you want to *ask* the interviewee, not *tell* him.

   As interviewee, if you are asked this type of question, you should expand on the reason for your answer. Assume you were asked to give an example of your analytical ability or to explain *why* you would be interested in working for a large company.

4. *Broad brush*   These are questions such as "Tell me about your work experience last summer." Once you have asked this type of question, do not allow the candidate to throw the question back to you by asking "What do you mean?" Instead, reply, "Tell me about anything you think is significant about that experience." A broad-brush question requires an interviewee to demonstrate an ability to think about a broad subject area, to choose what to include in his response, and to organize his thoughts.

   As interviewee, if you are genuinely unclear about a question, you should either ask the interviewer to clarify what he means or rephrase the question yourself to make sure you are answering it. For example, if an interviewer asks you "Tell me about your interests," you may reply, "Would you like to hear about my interests on the job, or outside?"

5. *Compare and contrast*   Questions that ask an interviewee to compare or contrast two situations, or to choose between two equally attractive alternatives can tell you about an interviewee's analytical and reasoning abilities. For example, you may ask a person who

has worked in two different, but related, jobs to compare his experiences in those jobs. Or, you may ask a candidate whether he would prefer to work on one major matter for an extended period of time or several smaller matters at once?

After a compare-and-contrast question, ask appropriate follow-up questions, such as, "Why do you prefer to work on several smaller matters?", "Can you give me an example of a situation in which you worked on several matters at once?", "How did you handle it?", "What did you do, say, etc.?", "Can you give me an example of a time you worked on one large matter?", "How did you handle it?" These types of questions force a candidate to analyze a situation in a different manner than a question that deals with only a single experience.

As interviewee, you may wish to compare prior-job experiences even if you are not specifically asked to do so. This may provide a more creative and interesting response to a question about one job, and may favorably impress the interviewer.

6. *Self-appraisal*   Self-appraisal questions force an interviewee to reflect on her own personality and abilities and will provide you with an opportunity to understand the interviewee as she sees herself. For example, if an interviewee is in the top 10 percent of her class, you may ask, "What do you think it is about you that allowed you to perform so well in school?" Depending upon the interviewee's answer, you may learn that the interviewee is (or at least perceives, or markets, herself as) hard working, intelligent, a good writer, or motivated. Without that question, you are merely guessing about what characteristic allowed the interviewee to achieve her success. You should then ask follow-up questions to elicit support

for the characteristics the interviewee has claimed to have.

By the way, note that you may also form some negative hypotheses about somebody who finishes in the top 10 percent of her class—that she is dull, one-dimensional, antisocial, etc. Of course, as with all hypotheses, you may be wrong. That's why you need to use the interview to explore your hypotheses with an open mind.

An interviewee who has prepared for interviews by assessing her own strengths and weaknesses will not be thrown by a self-appraisal question. Make sure that the response you give is one that you can support with specific examples.

7. *Multiple questions* Asking multiple questions at once only confuses the interviewee and makes it difficult for you to get the information you want. For example, do not ask a candidate, "Can you tell me about your job with X company, what your responsibilities were, any promotions you received, what you liked and disliked, and why you left?" Keep your questions simple—"How?", "When?", "What happened next?"

As interviewee, you should divide up a multiple question in order to avoid getting confused. In the above example, you might start your response with, "I'd be happy to. Perhaps we can start by describing my job and responsibilities with X company, and then I can address any other related questions you may have."

Specific Questions

Of course, there are a limitless number of questions you could ask a candidate. As is true in most aspects of interviewing, there is seldom a right or wrong question to ask in an interview. The exception, of course, is questions that are illegal, which are covered in more detail in "Achieving Diversity and Avoiding Discriminatory Questions."

Because there are often no right or wrong answers, however, does not mean that all questions are equally good (or bad). Some questions are more likely to elicit valuable information than others. Try the following interview-questions exercise and compare your answers with the comments I have made below. I recommend that you answer all questions first, then return to look at the comments below each question. By doing that, you will force yourself to take a position on each question and evaluate whether you agree with the comments.

For each of the following questions, indicate whether the question is:

> GOOD: it is legal and elicits quality information
> AVERAGE: it is legal, but may or may not be appropriate or elicit useful information
> POOR: it is illegal, inappropriate, or not useful in obtaining information

1. We've got a pretty team-oriented environment around here. To what extent do you like working on a team, and can you give me an example of a successful team experience?

_____ Good   _____ Average   _____ Poor

This question may give the interviewer some useful information regarding the interviewee's ability to work with a team, particularly because it asks for a specific example of a successful team experience. The problems with this question are that it telegraphs the answer the interviewer wants in the first sentence (The message to the interviewee is, "Do you like to work on a team, or should we end this interview right now?") and the second sentence asks several questions at once. A better way of asking for this information might be, "Do you prefer to work on your own, or as part of a team?" This formulation does not suggest what answer the interviewer is looking for. If the interviewee answers, "As part of a team," the interviewer might follow up with, "Can you give me an example of a successful team experience?"

2. Why do you think we should hire you?

_____ Good   _____ Average   _____ Poor

This question certainly gives the interviewee free reign to speak of her qualifications. The trouble is that the question may be overly broad and, in any case, may have a rather condescending tone to it, implying to the interviewee an attitude of "What makes you think you're good enough to be in the same room with me?" To me, it's a lazy and ineffective way of trying to get the interviewee to do your work for you. While your questions should be open-ended, they should provide some focus. "Tell me about yourself?" is not a good question.

3. I see from your resume that you are fluent in French. *Dites-moi—le programme que vous avez assisté á l'Université de Paris á Paris; est-ce que vous le recommendez?*

_____ Good   _____ Average   _____ Poor

This question will test the interviewee's honesty in listing on her resume that she is fluent in French. At the very least, a person who is unable to answer this question would have demonstrated poor judgment in listing fluency in French on her resume. Of course, if French is useful in the particular job, this question would also be a way of exploring the interviewee's capacity in that area.

The question shows the interviewer's interest in what was probably a significant experience for the interviewee. And, by demonstrating that the interviewer has an interest or ability common to the interviewee, i.e., speaking French, the question may also be a way of establishing rapport.

Some, however, find this question too much of a test of the interviewee, and therefore overly confrontational. (Note that the question could be made far more confrontational with a small change in the lead-in to, "So you say that you are fluent in French." It might have been made less confrontational with a lead-in such as, "It's been a long time since I had a chance to speak any French, would you mind if I try? *Dites-moi . . .*") The interviewee's reaction may depend upon the tone used in asking the question. Asked in a friendly tone, I see nothing wrong with the question. (Note: I distinguish between somebody who indicates that she is *fluent* in French and somebody who merely lists French as a language on her resume. I would find this approach more problematic with the latter.) The only thing that would tend to dissuade me from using it is that I do not speak French.

4. Can you give me an example of a situation that required you to work closely with someone with whom you've

disagreed or had a personality conflict? How did you deal with that?

_____ Good   _____ Average   _____ Poor

The information sought by this question is clearly relevant to most job situations which, in one way or another, may involve disagreements or personality conflicts. Also, because a particular situation is sought by the question, the interviewer is likely to get good, concrete information. (Asking "Can you give me an example of . . . ?" is an effective way of generating specific information.) This is not the type of question, however, that you would want to ask at the beginning of an interview, because it would be likely to put the interviewee on the defensive. It seems entirely appropriate, however, as a part of a discussion of an interviewee's prior-job experience.

5. Ask a black applicant: Why would you be interested in working for our company?

_____ Good   _____ Average   _____ Poor

The information sought by this question—why the interviewee is interested in your company—is perfectly appropriate. Chances are that the question is not illegal. The problem with the question, however, is that its phrasing implies some surprise by the interviewer that a black applicant would be interested in working for the company.

Even if you were to ask the identical question of all interviewees, the applicant may assume you are directing it at him because he is black. After all, he would not know you are asking it of everyone. As we shall see later in this book, it is the perception of the interviewee that is most important in the area of discriminatory questions, so you must consider how interviewees may react to your question. You could avoid the problem and get the same information with a slight rephrasing of the question, such as "Tell me how you came to be interested in working for our company."

6. If you were to be an animal, what type of animal would you be?

_____ Good   _____ Average   _____ Poor

Some interviewers think this type of question is valuable, because it gives them a sense of how quickly the interviewee can think on his feet. Interviewees, however, frequently find these types of questions either stupid or intended solely to produce stress.

Furthermore, if you develop what you think is a clever question and ask it of every interviewee, that question is going to get around extremely quickly. After you'd conducted several interviews on campus, a candid interviewee would walk into your interview room, hand extended, and say, "Hello, I'm a panther, what are you?"

One of my former partners used to think it clever to ask every interviewee, "Would it be relevant for me to ask you if you always stopped at stop signs when you drive?" After the first interviewee, every interviewee who came through the door knew he would be asked that question. That clever interview technique did not enhance the reputation of either my partner or the firm, nor, I suspect, did it give him particularly useful information. Try not to be too clever in your questions.

Finally, if you absolutely can't resist these clever questions (and *do* try), at least develop a half dozen of them, rotate them and explain to the interviewee your rationale for using them. In this way, you will keep your own interest up, you will prevent your questions from being passed on from interviewee to interviewee if you are seeing many candidates in a row, and, by explaining your rationale, you may make the questions seem less objectionable to the interviewee.

7. I see from your resume that you participate in the minority outreach program. In what way have you been involved in that program?

_____ Good   _____ Average   _____ Poor

This question is perfectly appropriate because it asks about an interviewee's experience in a program she has mentioned on her resume. Some interviewers, concerned about avoiding discriminatory questions, may refrain from asking questions that are perfectly appropriate of a minority candidate. (Indeed, note that from the resume item alone, you do not know whether the candidate is even a minority candidate.) Do not avoid asking minority candidates about experiences they have had merely because those experiences involve minority groups.

One small point: I'd stay away from using the phrase, "I see from your resume that . . ." You don't have to tell the interviewee what is on her resume; she prepared it, so she knows. Also, interviewers who use this phrase tend to be looking down at the resume as they say it, thus not maintaining good eye contact with the interviewee. Instead, just look the interviewee in the eye and say, "I'd like to hear about your job at . . .''

8. I see you're a butterfly collector. Tell me about what you've enjoyed in butterfly collecting?

_____ Good   _____ Average   _____ Poor

This question shows interest in a hobby the interviewee participates in. As such, it may be a good way of establishing rapport with the interviewee. It is not a threatening area of inquiry so it also may help to relax the interviewee if asked near the beginning of the interview.

Beyond that, you may even learn some useful information relating to the job. For example, a person who collects butterflies may show great attention to detail, may have shown breadth of interest or curiosity by studying not only about butterflies, but about areas in which they are found, may have participated in a club relating to the activity, sold portions of his collection for profit, etc. Of course, none of this may be the case, but unless you ask, you will never know.

9. At times it is necessary for employees at the company to work on weekends. What would you do if you were scheduled to be in a friend's wedding and a senior officer asked you to work over the weekend on an important client project?

_____ Good   _____ Average   _____ Poor

Though it may be important for you to know how hard an interviewee is willing to work, the answer you will likely get to a hypothetical question like this one is the interviewee's guess as to what answer you are looking for. Furthermore, the question sends a rather unfavorable message to the interviewee about the company because the interviewee will assume that this situation is likely to arise. So it is almost as if you said, "Welcome to our company, how would you like to miss your friend's wedding?"

You could get the information you are looking for more effectively by asking the interviewee whether she had ever experienced a conflict between a job demand and a personal commitment and how she handled that. Still other ways of approaching the subject would be to explore the interviewee's typical work week, or to ask her whether she had ever held a job that required her to work hard, and then ask her to describe what that entailed. In any case, this is a topic you would not want to explore early in the interview.

10. I'm really interested in your thesis on "The Relationship between Mathematical and Philosophical Approaches to the Concept of Value." What were your principal conclusions?

_____ Good   _____ Average   _____ Poor

Many interviewers avoid this type of question, either because they are not interested in the topic or because they feel they may not understand the answer. Most interviewers like to feel that they are in control, so they avoid questions the interviewee may know far more about than they do.

Try not to fall into that trap. Show interest and curiosity in topics that your interviewee has shown interest in. And remember that many jobs require an employee to explain something to a customer, client, or coworker who does not understand much about what the employee is explaining. An interviewee's ability to explain a complicated thesis in a manner that is understandable to you may well be a good predictor of his ability to perform a similar duty on the job.

Prefacing a question with, "I'm really interested in . . ." is a good approach. It makes an interviewee feel good to hear that the interviewer is interested in something on his resume, and will encourage him to be open in his response.

11. Tell me about your job waiting tables at Café du Paris.

_____ Good   _____ Average   _____ Poor

This question is perfectly appropriate because it inquires about a prior job experience. Even assuming that the job the interviewee is applying for seems remote from waiting on tables at a restaurant, elements of the waiting experience may be quite relevant to a person's on-the-job behavior. For example, waiting tables may entail balancing many tasks at once, dealing with rude customers, an ability to deal with pressure and an ability to tolerate routine tasks. All of these characteristics may be valuable in even high-level positions. The waiting job may also have been a part-time job during school and therefore may demonstrate motivation on the part of the interviewee, and may also be evidence of the interviewee's ability to balance a number of conflicting time demands at once. Of course, if the interviewee has many other job experiences on her resume, an interviewer may choose not to inquire about the job waiting tables, or at least not devote too much time to it.

"Tell me about . . . ?" is an excellent way to begin a question. That form of question invites a story from the interviewee, and often elicits a valuable response.

12. What are your greatest strengths?

_____ Good _____ Average _____ Poor

This is the type of question that is routinely asked by many interviewers, perhaps because they were asked it so often when they were interviewing. It tends to elicit a rather rehearsed response. When followed up with a series of questions that explore specific instances in which the interviewee's strengths are displayed it may produce useful information. By itself, though, it's average, at best.

13. I really admire what you have accomplished. Were you born blind, or did you become blind later in life?

_____ Good _____ Average _____ Poor

This interviewer may well be trying to show sincere interest in the interviewee. Nonetheless, the question is illegal under the Americans with Disabilities Act, and should not be asked in an interview.

General Principles for Interviewers

What general principles can the prospective interviewer draw from this exercise?

1. In most cases, you need to make up your own mind whether a particular question is a good one—there is no right or wrong answer. If you find the question interesting and the information you are likely to get from it valuable, ask the question; otherwise, do not.

2. You should avoid certain questions, however, because they stand a high risk of being considered illegal. This topic is discussed in much greater detail in chapter 13.

3. Whether a question is a good, average, or poor question may depend on the tone of an interviewer's voice in asking it, the look on his face as he asks it, the particular way the question is phrased or the point in the interview when the question is asked. You need to become sensitive to these subtle factors.

4. Whether you decide to ask a question on a particular topic on the interviewee's resume may depend in part on what else is on that resume. You may pass up asking a question about waiting tables on a resume of a person who has had many other interesting job experiences. With another candidate's resume, you might be dying for something as interesting as waiting tables to talk about.

5. In deciding what questions to ask, don't be guided by what *you* were asked as a candidate for a position. Chances are good that the interviewer who interviewed you had not given a great amount of thought to the questions he asked. Asking the questions you were asked is likely to perpetuate playing the interview game.

6. Don't be afraid to ask questions on topics that you may know little about. At least you'll be able to determine whether the interviewee can formulate his answer in a way you can understand.

7. You may learn extremely valuable information about a

candidate from an experience or interest the candidate has that is seemingly quite remote from the job for which the candidate is interviewing. (Remember the butterfly collector.)

In general, one of the most important characteristics an interviewer can possess is genuine curiosity. Don't be afraid to vary your interviews. Talk about something new with each interviewee. (Try coming away from each interview with some new information that you might "drop" at the next cocktail party you attend.) Not only are you more likely to listen to something new, you are also less likely to get pat answers.

If you try to learn about the particular interviewee in front of you, rather than reciting a stock list of questions, you are far more likely to conduct an effective interview. A series of interviews in which you are just going through the motions is boring both for you and for the interviewee. A rule of thumb I try to apply in formulating interview questions is that if I'm asking a question I could be asking of *every* interviewee, chances are good it is not a question I want to ask of *any* interviewee.

If you want to test a particular question, ask yourself whether it is:

- specific to the candidate
- based on the candidate's past experience
- open-ended
- nondiscriminatory
- job-related
- nonleading

If the answer to each of these six questions is "yes," chances are you're asking a good question.

Lessons for Interviewees

What should interviewees take from this chapter?

1. Many interviewers ask routine questions because they don't know any better. Of course, you must be prepared to answer those questions. But you may do the interviewer (and yourself) a favor by steering the interviewer gently toward more fruitful, less hackneyed, territory.

2. Don't worry when an interviewer spends time talking about experiences or interests on your resume that may seem somewhat remote from the job for which you are applying. An experienced interviewer may be getting extremely useful information from this discussion.

3. Though I don't want to condone offensive questions, interviewees should understand that most often those questions are asked out of ignorance rather than out of any intention to discriminate. Indeed, those questions are often asked out of genuine (though perhaps inappropriate or misguided) interest in the interviewee. Unless a question is truly offensive to you, you would do well to assume that the question is asked for benign purposes, and not overreact. Of course, the offensiveness of a particular question will vary from one interviewee to another. If the question is blatantly and seriously offensive to you, there is no reason not to let the interviewer know that you object to the question.

4. Anything you put on your resume is fair territory for an interviewer to explore. If you're not prepared to talk about the senior thesis you wrote in college, don't list it on your resume.

5. Don't overstate your case on the resume, even in an apparently innocuous way.

I remember the time I interviewed a second-year law student from the University of Chicago who had listed as one of his hobbies "expert on Brooklyn Dodger trivia." I knew that one of my partners knew an awful lot about the old Dodgers, so, shortly after the interview began, I told the interviewee, "C'mon, we're going down to see Quaini."

The two of us marched downstairs to my partner's office and I said, "This fella says he's an expert on Brooklyn Dodger trivia, Duane; why don't you see if he is?" The first question my partner asked him was "Who was the organist at Ebbets Field?" The interviewee responded with a blank stare. To make matters worse for the interviewee, I happened to know the answer—Gladys Gooding.

I don't think the interviewee ever recovered from being exposed as a "fraud." He did not receive an offer from my firm.

If your interviewer believes that you have misrepresented one of your credentials, you can forget about receiving an offer from that company. She will question your honesty in general, and will probably assume that you have misrepresented other credentials, as well.

6. Give an interviewer as wide an area to ask questions about, and as much of an opportunity to establish rapport with you, as possible by including as many diverse experiences and interests on your resume as you can. Keep your resume to one page, though. Be willing to sacrifice items such as "career objective," "date and place of birth," "high school education" and even "references" in favor of including more interests, activities, and job experiences.

SEVEN

QUESTIONS AN INTERVIEWEE SHOULD CONSIDER ASKING

Thus far we've looked at questions primarily from the interviewer's standpoint. The interview, though, is designed to permit the interviewee to gather information, as well. Indeed, as the hiring process progresses, the interviewee becomes as much the information gatherer as the information giver.

I hesitate to provide a list of questions, for either party. My fear is that some readers may memorize the list, and use it indiscriminately. Please don't do that. You will bore both yourself and the interviewer. You should not ask any question unless you are sincerely interested in the answer.

In considering the questions suggested below, interviewees should recognize that some may be inappropriate at certain stages in the interview process. In general, the further the interview process has progressed, the more probing your questions may appropriately become.

Many of the questions contain natural subparts or follow-up questions; I have indicated those additional questions as well. Finally, where it might not otherwise be clear, I explain why I think the question may be important for an interviewee to ask.

In any case, here are fifteen questions interviewees should consider asking:

1. *What will my duties be?* Don't be taken in by a title or a general job description. You don't spend your days being "an assistant vice-president" or "providing support to senior officers." You spend time photocopying documents, dictating reports of daily staff meetings, etc. Find out *specifically* what you will do. Ask how people spend their time on the job. You may want to ask this question of both the person who would be your supervisor and people who are working in similar positions. Comparing their answers may prove instructive.

2. *With whom will I work?* No matter how exciting the job may seem, your own satisfaction is likely to be governed largely by those you will have day-to-day contact with. A lousy boss, co-worker, or subordinate can make the most exciting job into a veritable hell. You should be interested both in those who will be working as your supervisors, as your colleagues and, if applicable, under your supervision. You will want to speak with representatives of each group to gauge what it will be like to work with those people.

3. *To whom will I report?* Your ability to succeed in your company may depend largely on the person to whom you report, and how he fits into the company's structure. This is particularly important if you view this as a long-term position in which you hope to advance. In many companies (not all), simply being terrific will not help much if you do not have

access to the right people. Find out how the person you report to fits into the organizational scheme at the company. If there is more than one person to whom you report, get this information for each person.

4. *How will my performance be evaluated?* This is an extremely important question because it will govern your pay and possible promotions. This question suggests several sub-questions. You need to know the standards by which you will be judged, who will judge you, at what intervals you will be judged, and how the evaluation process will be conducted. You may want to ask to see the evaluation form that will be used in evaluating your performance.

5. *What are the opportunities for advancement?* In addition to asking about the opportunities, you may want to know when advancement may occur and what advancement will be based on. Will it depend solely on your performance, on the performance of a group you are a part of, or on the performance of the entire company? If it depends on the group or the company, you will need to assess their strength. Is there room for advancement? Are all the positions above you filled with relatively young people who have no place above them to move?

6. *Where have people who left the position I am interviewing for gone?* This will give you some sense of what the future holds for people in this job. You may also wish to ask why those people left and whether you may talk with them. If you have the opportunity to talk to some of them, do. At the same time, though, be aware that people who leave a company sometimes have axes to grind and may be judging the company unfairly.

A related question is how high the turnover rate

has been. If the rate has been high, e.g., people have been leaving the position in significant numbers, this suggests there may be problems in the position or with the supervision you may receive. Explore the reasons for the turnover.

7. *What are the three most important goals of the company?* If the company is a diverse, mega-company, you may wish to reduce the scope of this question to a division or unit. You will want to know whether these goals are consistent with your own goals and values. You should be interested not only in the substance of the answer, but also in whether people are able to answer the question at all. If people are unable to answer it, the company may lack clarity in its goals or communication within the company may be poor. Either would be reason for concern.

8. *What are the three most important goals of the person to whom I will report?* You should ask this question both of the person to whom you would report and also to others who work for her. As with company goals, you will want to check for consistency with your own goals and values. Again, you should be interested not only in the substance of the remarks, but in whether people can formulate answers to this question at all and in the consistency of their answers.

9. *What is the most important thing to you personally about the company?* The answer will give you some insight both into the characteristics of the company and into the values of the person to whom you are speaking. This should help you determine how you might fit into the culture. If the answer you get is general or vague, don't hesitate to ask a follow-up question requesting clarification.

10. *What characteristics does it take to succeed in this position?* You will be able to tell from this answer

whether people at the company have considered this question. If they have not, your advancement may depend upon your good fortune, or upon the good graces of supervisors. To the extent that the company has assessed the characteristics necessary to succeed, you can consider whether your strengths are consistent with what the position requires.

11. *What characteristics cause people to fail in this position?* The answer should not just be the flip side of the answer to question number ten. If you have some of the characteristics that cause people to fail, consider looking elsewhere for a job.

12. *What are the two or three greatest challenges the company faces in the next year?* You will probably want to follow up this question with similar questions with regard to the department in which you will be working and your particular job. You will want to note how these challenges relate to one another. You may also want to ask what strategies and steps the company and department are taking to meet those challenges. The answers to these questions may help you assess the future prospects of the company and how your skills may contribute to them.

13. *I have some interests outside of work, including [name one or two]. Will I be able to pursue these interests and still do the kind of job expected of me?* You may want to follow this with questions about how one can maintain the proper balance between work and outside life. You may also ask specifically what outside interests the person you are speaking to pursues because that is likely to be a better test of whether one can really pursue those interests than a general response about company policy. Ask whether the interviewer has had to cancel any vacations he's

planned in the past few years because of company business.

14. *If he/she were highly motivated and talented, what could somebody hope to accomplish in this job?* This question is related to the earlier questions about the duties and opportunities for advancement, but it goes beyond those questions. It suggests you are achievement oriented and willing to stretch; that you may be that highly motivated and talented person.

15. *Do you have any further questions about my qualifications for the job?* If you get an honest answer to this question, you may be able to address some lingering doubts the interviewer holds about you.

All of the above are intelligent and important questions, and should mark you as a rather sophisticated candidate. I want to emphasize once again, though, that you should not memorize this list and ask these questions of each interviewer. Ask only those questions you truly care about. Don't try to win the interview game by asking twenty penetrating questions. Though some interviewers may be impressed by the quality of an interviewee's questions, most interviewers dread wasting time with the ritual question-and-answer dance almost as much as interviewees do. And experienced interviewers can generally spot candidates who are trotting out questions just for show.

I have not included in this list any financially oriented questions—for example, questions about the financial condition of the company, or about what your salary would be, or what bonuses and benefits may be available. Of course, all of these are legitimate and important questions.

With respect to salary and benefits, your approach should differ depending upon the level of the position you are interviewing for. For a more senior position, you may want to raise the issue rather early on. If you and the employer are not within range as to salary, there's no sense in either of you wasting much time. In more junior positions, you should generally wait to raise the question at least until after the initial interview or round of interviews, since your early focus should be on the job and the training and opportunities it presents. Once you are beyond the initial stages, though, there is nothing wrong with asking directly what the salary and benefits will be. The question may seem uncomfortable to you, but it is perfectly appropriate. After all, the employer does not expect you to work for nothing. The salary question for the interviewee is rather like the grades question for the interviewer; awkward, perhaps, but one that both sides recognize will and should be asked.

I've also not included in this chapter questions that may be personally important to certain interviewees, such as travel requirements of the job, or the possibility or likelihood of a move to another city. You will need to augment the questions suggested here with others that may be particularly important to you personally.

EIGHT

THE WORST QUESTIONS EMPLOYERS ASK: Why They're Bad and How to Handle Them

From time to time I have asked recent graduates to identify the worst questions they were asked during an interview season. I have found a remarkable consistency in the response I get, both from year to year and from one type of student (college, law, business, etc.) to another. Listed below are twenty of the most common worst questions, together with my comments and suggestions. (By the way, I have found I can compile almost the identical list by asking senior interviewers at a company what their *favorite* questions are.)

The consistency with which these questions pop up suggests that interviewees can expect to be asked many of them during your job search. So you ought to be prepared to answer them—as well as other equally unimaginative or offensive questions. The comments below should help you understand why interviewers ask these questions. With that understanding, you will be able to respond directly to their concerns. In some cases, I also suggest ways you might approach answering a particular question. Because many of the questions are so banal, though, it becomes difficult to come up with interesting or creative answers.

Interviewers should consider how routinely you ask these questions. Do you get answers that are genuinely useful? If not, why do you continue to ask those questions? Are there better ways for you to get at the information you are seeking?

1. *Why did you go to [law/business/graduate] school?* Interviewers who ask this question are seeking some insight into the candidate's motivation. What they usually get is a variation on one of the following themes: "I've always wanted to go to _____," "I was inspired by some hero or family member to go to _____," "I think my talents are particularly well suited to _____," "I have always found _____ fascinating."

Rarely does an interviewer get an answer something like, "Gee, I wasn't quite sure what I wanted to do, and this seemed interesting/like something that would give me good experience or flexibility." Many interviewers would think that answer shows a lack of motivation. What it really would show is (perhaps an excess of) honesty.

If the "I wasn't quite sure . . ." answer is your honest response as an interviewee, you will have to choose between candor and playing the interview game. There is no doubt that candor carries risks. With most interviewers, you would be safer giving one of the canned responses that interviewees typically make. However, you might consider instead giving a response something like the following: "I wish I could tell you that I wanted to go to law school since reading about Abraham Lincoln in third grade, but that's not true. The fact is, I wasn't sure exactly what I wanted to do after college. Law seemed interesting, and something that would give me a lot of flexibility. Now, since I got to law school . . ." That kind of answer would win a lot of points with me as an interviewer, but it might not be as well received by many other interviewers.

2. *Why do you want to be a [lawyer/accountant/computer programmer/sales manager/investment banker]?* This question is similar to number one, but is more specific about the interviewee's interest. Again, the interviewer is typically testing the interviewee's motivation and commitment to a particular career, and seeking to gauge whether the interviewee has realistic expectations about what he will encounter in that career.

3. *Why did you go to [name] school?* The interviewer wants to learn something about the interviewee's decision-making process, and, perhaps, get some sense of the individual's commitment to a particular geographical area. Interviewers like to see some serious thought given to the choice of school. Typical responses fall into these categories: "It was the best school I could get into," "I wanted to be at school in the _____ area, because that is the place I would like to work," "I have some good friends/relatives who went to _____ school and recommended it highly to 'me," "_____ school has a particularly strong department in (field)," "_____ school offered me the most financial assistance." I find all of these answers to be of limited use so I do not ask question.

Sometimes an interviewer will ask this question in a tone that suggests that the school the interviewee is attending is second-rate. Interviewees should not be apologetic about not attending an elite school. Being apologetic will be taken by interviewers as indicating a lack of self-confidence. The greater problem this apologetic stance creates is a mindset in the interviewee that assumes he has two strikes against him going into the interview. This cannot help but adversely affect the interviewee's performance in other respects as well. (Indeed, though I have focused here on the school, being overly apologetic about most anything—a poor grade, lack of experience in a particular area—will have the same affect.)

4. *Where do you see yourself [five, ten, seven-and-a-quarter] years from now?* Many interviewers regard this as a penetrating question—at least until I ask them what they get out of asking it. Though some interviewers think they get revealing information, most find they get rather prepared responses geared to what the interviewee thinks the interviewer wants to hear.

This question is meant to gauge the interviewee's motivation and the reasonableness of her career expectations. The honest answer to the question for most interviewees would be, "I have no idea." The expected response for most interviewers is that the interviewee will be progressing in his career at the company, learning new things, undertaking new responsibilities, etc.

For most interviewers, an indication that the interviewee plans to use the position for which he is interviewing as a stepping-stone to a position with another company or in another arena would be a serious negative, notwithstanding the fact that such an answer would demonstrate both a high degree of honesty and of motivation. Many interviewers seem to be looking for the interviewee (reported in a Robert Half International survey) who said that, if he were hired, he would demonstrate his loyalty by having the corporate logo tattooed on his forearm.

Once again, an interviewee will have to balance his desire to be candid with his willingness to play the interview game, in which complete candor carries risks.

5. *Why do you want to come to [city]?* Answers to this question range from people who grew up in the city or went to school there and want to return (or remain) there to answers that flatter the cosmopolitan nature or lifestyle of the interviewer's city to answers that indicate that a great aunt of the interviewee, long since deceased, once mentioned that she'd heard this was a pretty decent city to live in. A better question for an interviewer seeking to determine the level of the interviewee's interest in the city is, "Which cities are you interviewing in?" Assuming a truthful answer, the interviewer will get some sense of the interviewee's commitment to a particular city. A candidate who professes to be committed to New York, but is also interviewing with companies in Boston, Denver, Chicago, Miami, Sacramento, and Dubuque has a serious credibility problem.

6. *What can I tell you about the company? [Asked at the beginning of an interview.]* This question is almost universally regarded by interviewees as signaling the end of the interview. From the point that question is asked until the end of the interview, the interviewer generally learns little else about the interviewee. Indeed, inviting questions too early in the interview is the easiest and most common way

of turning over control of an interview to the interviewee.

As an interviewee, you should not assume that the interviewer has given up on you when she asks if you have questions. In fact, the invitation to ask questions may mean the interviewer believes she can learn a lot about you by the nature of the questions you ask. (I believe this confidence is misplaced. Many interviewees have been prepped to ask highly intelligent questions, the answers to which they cannot begin to comprehend.) It may also mean the interviewer has a strong interest in you and feels that by answering your questions, she will be able to sell you on the company.

Of course, the opposite also may be true, as well. The interviewer may have no interest in you, and inviting questions may be an easy way of consuming the interview time.

Confronted with the invitation to pose questions, the interviewee has a number of options. If you have some genuine questions you wish to have answered, ask them. If not, you may wish to turn the conversation back into a discussion of your qualifications by saying something like, "I've read quite a bit about the company and I think I have a pretty good sense of what I need to know at this point. Is there something else I can tell you about me?" Another alternative would be to ask a question about the interviewer. For one thing, this would show some interest in the interviewer, thus helping to establish rapport with him. It may also help you to learn something about the type of people who work at the company.

7. *Why do you want to work for this company?* This question is similar to numbers two and three

brought down to the company level. Again employers are looking for the interviewee's motivation, commitment, and decision-making process.

The most common response from interviewees amounts to, "Because I have a strong interest in an area the company is strong in." Many interviewees use this question as an opportunity to show the interviewer that they have done some homework by mentioning things about the company they have learned in preparing for the interview. Others use this as an opportunity for abject flattery by reciting to the interviewer what a wonderful company he represents. Rarely does an interviewer get what may be the most honest replies, including "because I need a job and this place seems as good as any," or "I'm not sure since I haven't worked here, why don't you tell me?"

I suppose that some interviewers may see value in asking this question because the answer may show the extent of the interviewee's preparation for the interview. That preparation may reflect on her motivation, her level of interest in the company, and how she approaches a task. If that's the goal, though, I don't understand why the interviewer does not ask the interviewee directly, "What did you do to prepare for this interview?"

8. *If we gave you a job, what would you bring to our company? What makes you special among so many qualified applicants?* Both of these questions are variations of "Tell me your qualifications." The second is rather condescending in tone. This question should be an easy lob to smash back for any interviewee who has prepared properly for an interview because he will have identified his strengths and how they fit with the position he is seeking.

9. *What's the best course you've taken in school, and why?*   Interviewers who ask this question are either looking for areas of interest that the interviewee may have or they want to determine what turns the interviewee on, the professor or the substance of a course. Interviewees may want to consider coming up with an unusual (but honest) answer such as, "I'd say it was my introduction to music course. I'd never been exposed to classical music before. Twenty years from now I probably won't remember who won the Peloponnesian War, but I think I'll continue to enjoy the pieces I learned to appreciate in that course."

Another problem with this question is that it's phrased in the singular ("What was the *best* course . . ."). By asking a question in this way, you may inhibit a response by implying that the interviewee can only choose one. By phrasing the question in the plural ("Which courses have you particularly enjoyed?"), you would make it easier for an interviewee to answer and to keep the flow of the interview going. And you accomplish the same purpose because the interviewee will almost invariably single out the best course in his response.

As interviewee, if you are asked to identify "the best" or "your favorite," you may reply in one of three ways: (a) if you have a "best" or "favorite," readily in mind, you may reply directly, (b) if you do not, you may pause to think about what would be your "best" or "favorite," and then reply, or (c) you may say, "Actually, there were several courses I liked . . ." and reply with several examples. As you reply, you may formulate a "best" or "favorite." If so, you may close the answer by saying, "I suppose, if I had to pick a 'best' or 'favorite,' it would be . . ."

10. *What was your worst grade in school/how do you explain X grade?* This may be a threatening question for an interviewee. On the other hand, you can look at it as an opportunity to explain a problem you may have had. Better that the interviewer ask the question than rule you out because of the grade.

Interviewees should be aware that many interviewers will view an answer that you did not work hard in the course because the subject matter did not interest you as an indication you may not be willing to do a task that needs to be done in your job, if it is not one that captures your imagination. Similarly, placing the blame on the professor may be taken as indicating you are unable to work well with people you do not particularly like. Were I to ask this question (which I would not) the answer that I would like best would be, "I just couldn't understand the material."

11. *What's your worst quality?* Some interviewers evidently expect the interviewee to come clean and admit serious shortcomings. In fact, what normally happens is that interviewees respond with a strength, such as "I work too hard" or "I expect too much of other people" or "I am a perfectionist" or "I get impatient when others waste time." This is rather transparent, but perhaps no worse than people who ask the question deserve. A slightly better way for an interviewer to approach this question is to ask for areas in which the interviewee feels he could improve, rather than asking directly for weaknesses.

A far better way for an interviewer to explore a candidate's weaknesses is to inquire into specific situations in which the interviewee was not satisfied with the way things turned out, wished things had turned out differently, had some problems, or was frustrated. By learning what the interviewee did (or didn't do) in those situations, an interviewer will be able to identify a candidate's weaknesses.

An interviewee who is asked what his weaknesses are will have to decide whether to play the interview game by disguising a strength as a weakness, or reply with a real weakness. To some interviewers, admitting a weakness will be taken as a sign of strength, showing a certain humility, candor, and self-confidence. Other interviewers may use the information you provide to rule you out. If you do discuss a weakness, you may also want to indicate to the interviewer how you are dealing with it. For example, "I sometimes have trouble balancing a lot of different tasks. I'm taking a time-management course in the evenings, though, which should help me with that." (Or "I often have this strong urge to strangle my boss, but I'm thinking about going for counseling help in a few months.")

Finally, an interviewee may want to try a bit of humor in response to the weaknesses question. One recent graduate I interviewed told me she got so sick of answering the question of what her worst characteristic was that she finally answered, "I over-pack." I'd have hired her in a second.

12. *So tell me about yourself.* This is a more general form of question number eight. Here, in addition to asking what you would bring to the job, interviewers may be looking for how you organize and focus your answer to this question. Interviewees probably would be best advised not to begin their answer with a discussion of which hospital they were born in and the trauma they experienced in emerging from the womb (although, come to think of it, if I

were mistakenly to ask this question, I would rather appreciate the humor inherent in that response).

13. *If you were going to Mars and could take three things with you, what would they be?* The interviewer who asks this (or similar) question(s) fancies himself an extremely creative questioner and will read deep meaning and significance into the answers he receives. Some interviewers who ask this question are adherents of the stress-interview technique. Others simply want to see how an interviewee approaches an off-the-wall question such as this. I'd be inclined to respond with an off-the-wall answer, such as "a Mars bar, an American Express card, and a return ticket to Dubuque," or with a question, such as "how long would I be gone?" Either of those responses, though, would probably doom me to failure with the interviewer who considered this a sensible question.

Off-the-wall questions are not limited to trips to Mars. A friend of mine told me he asked a fellow who had listed golf as an interest, "If you could be any golf club you wanted, which club would it be?" His answer was the same as my friend's—a six iron—and for the same reason (you can do many things with a six). My friend reported that the interviewee received an offer. I wonder how the candidate would have fared had he responded, "A driver, because I like to pound the hell out of things" or "A putter, because I like to get a big reward for very little effort."

14. *What do you think of [a particular candidate's] chances for reelection if the economy doesn't improve [or a question about another controversial issue]?* The interviewer who asks this question may genuinely

be interested in discussing a matter of political or philosophical import. This type of question may make the interviewee uneasy, though, since the controversial and/or emotional nature of it makes it stressful. These questions also may send a message to the interviewee that a particular political preference is important in the job setting. For those reasons, interviewers may be well advised to stay away from this kind of question. Not everything you might like to discuss with an employee over drinks *after* he has been hired is a wise topic for discussion during the interview process. (Of course, if the interviewee's resume indicated he had been active in that candidate's first election campaign, that would be a reason to ask this question.)

15. *You have recently died. What does your obituary say?* This question may be geared to assess the interviewee's motivation, goals, and values, and also her particular strengths. It is a combination of questions four and twelve, but asks about her perception of what *others* value about her. This question does allow for some creativity. You may want to suggest that the answer depends on who the author of the obit was. It's probably wise not to dissolve into tears at the prospect of your death.

16. *What question could I ask that would really intimidate you?* This is obviously a stress question, especially if it is followed up by asking the question that the interviewee recites in response to the question. Several options appear to be open to the interviewee, including: "The question you just asked," "Nothing, I don't intimidate easily," or "What answer, if I gave it to you, would really intimidate you?" Many interviewers would find those responses too cheeky, however, so you may simply choose to reply with a

question that has been asked of you in the past which had the described affect.

17. *What does your father do?* This question may be asked out of genuine curiosity about your family, or out of some sense that your family connections may be relevant to your business potential. Though curiosity about what a candidate has done is desirable, curiosity about his personal life has no place in the job interview. Conduct an *individualized* interview, but not a *personal* one. Many minority candidates think these types of personal questions are asked of them and not of white candidates. It is not an appropriate question.

However, as an interviewee, if you sense that it is asked out of curiosity you may wish simply to respond. If you are offended by the question, tell the interviewer that you do not regard this as an appropriate question, since it does not bear upon your qualifications for the position.

18. *Are you married or single?* This may be asked out of genuine curiosity or for discriminatory purposes. It is clearly illegal, and I suggest you so inform anybody who asks that question. You may choose to preface your response with, "Though I'm sure you do not intend to offend anybody . . ."

19. *Why did you wait so long to go to [business/law/ medical/graduate] school?* This question is generally asked of second-career people. It is really a variant of question number two, "Why do you want to be a . . . ?," and seems implicitly to question the motivation of the second-career person. That's ironic, because a person who has given up one career to pursue another has shown strong motivation. In any case, the phrasing of the above question is clearly offensive, and may arguably be illegal.

20. *Are you intending to have children?*   This question is similar to question eighteen but is almost certainly being asked for an illegal purpose. I would let the interviewer know that this question is not permissible.

These twenty questions fall into patterns. They tend to fit into the following five categories (note that some questions may fall into more than one category and, of course, not everybody would agree that they should be placed into the categories I've created):

(a) hackneyed (1 through 11)
(b) confrontational (3, 8, 10, 11, 13 through 16, 19)
(c) overly broad (12)
(d) illegal (17, 18, 19, 20)
(e) stupid (4, 13, 15)

Except for illegal questions, individual interviewers may differ as to whether these "worst" questions are worth asking. I must confess, for example, that when I used to interview, I sometimes liked to try to catch students a little off guard. To that end, I used to occasionally ask law students whether they thought students should be allowed to type their law school exams. You'd be surprised at the Socratic dialogue that may ensue on that topic. The discussion often sounds something like this:

> "Do you type your exams?"
> "What?"
> "I asked whether you type your exams."
> "No, I don't, why?"
> "Do you think it's fair that people are allowed to type their exams?"
> "Sure, if they can type, more power to them."

"But doesn't that give them an unfair advantage?"

"I don't necessarily think that the more you put down, the better the grade you get."

"Well, I suppose that's right. But do you think it would be fair to give one person ten minutes more to answer a question than another?"

"No."

"But, in effect, isn't that what you're doing by allowing one person to type and another not to? If one person can put something down physically much faster than another, aren't you really giving the typist extra time to think about his answer?"

"You're not prohibiting anybody from typing. Anybody can do it. So if somebody has that skill, let him use it. Some people can think faster than others. And what about the poor professor who has to grade the papers? Typing makes it much easier to read."

"But aren't law school exams supposed to test skills that are relevant to the practice of law, and is typing relevant? I suggest that dictating is a lot more relevant to practicing law than typing, but nobody allows students to dictate their exams. And as to making it easier on the professor, why not let everybody type the exam—afterward, from the handwritten one. A spot check of the written against the typed versions could be conducted and anybody found cheating would be booted out of school."

Believe it or not, the discussion can go on from there. For example, one could ask if word processors should be allowed. Or private secretaries. One could also explore whether permitting typewriters or word processors is a form of economic discrimination, favoring those who can afford the technology.

I'm certainly not suggesting that all interviewers go out and harangue students about typing their exams. This interview technique may strike you as a bit frivolous, even as evidence that I was put out to pasture just before I would have otherwise been confined to an institution. (I have a theory that there are a limited number of candidates an interviewer can speak to in a lifetime. Most experienced interviewers exceed that number before they retire from their hiring responsibilities.) However, these questions at least allow you to judge how quickly the person can think on her feet (or, more accurately, seat) about something that she has encountered for the first time and how well she can defend her initial position or, where appropriate, yield. And I tried to pose these questions in a good-natured manner, and used the technique only occasionally.

In any case, most of the twenty worst questions listed above show no particular interest in the interviewee as a person because they could be asked of any interviewee. I would suggest that unless, as an interviewer, you genuinely find the answers to the above questions illuminating and helpful, you try to avoid all of these questions, and others like them. Because of the predictable nature of many of the questions and the expected responses, they encourage the interviewee to play the interview game, rather than to convey useful information.

Interviewees should be prepared to answer these questions honestly, addressing the underlying concern of the interviewer. You should also give some thought as to how to convert some of these rather deadly questions into more interesting ones. One approach might be to explore with the interviewer why he is asking the question. Another would be to come up with an unusual answer to the question, such as that suggested above to question nine. Finally, consider using humor, but be aware that not all interviewers have my (warped) sense of humor. So using humor carries its risks.

NINE

ANSWERING QUESTIONS

An interview involves an *exchange* of information. So both the interviewer and the interviewee must understand not only how to *elicit* information, but also how to *convey* it.

Until now, we have concentrated primarily on how to elicit information—by making the other person comfortable, by using the resume effectively, by asking good questions, and by avoiding bad questions. In this chapter, we will try to identify what makes a good answer. As you will see, the same elements go into an effective answer, regardless of which side of the table you sit on. Here are ten guidelines that will help both interviewers and interviewees improve the quality of their answers.

1. *Answer the question that's asked.* This principle seems so basic you would think it doesn't need to be repeated, but it does. For one thing, as pointed out earlier in this book, some experts on interviewing advise interviewees who want to avoid answering

a question simply to answer a different question, ignoring the one that is asked. I think that is poor advice because it assumes the interviewer is dumb enough not to recognize that his question was not answered. Anybody who didn't answer questions I asked didn't get hired.

Apart from *intentionally* not answering the question that is asked, though, interviewers and interviewees often do that without meaning to. Either they do not listen to the question, or they do not understand it. Their answer, then, comes across as unresponsive and marks them either as not very bright or evasive, neither of which, of course, helps them achieve their objectives in the interview. If you are unsure about the question, ask the other person to repeat it. Or paraphrase the question yourself to test whether you've understood it.

2. *Show respect for the questioner.*   This is important because both the interviewer and interviewee want to gain the other's admiration (either to obtain a desirable offer or to encourage a qualified candidate to accept an offer). And when is the last time you admired somebody who did not respect you?

Consider every question to be worthy of your attention. That may not be so easy for interviewees confronted with some of the worst questions discussed in the last chapter. But remember that if you treat a question as silly or irrelevant, you are treating the questioner as silly or irrelevant, as well.

On the other hand, if you indicate "that's a good question" or "that's an interesting question," you are complimenting the questioner. Of course, you should not use these complimentary phrases repeatedly during the interview; nor should you ever use them unless you truly mean it. Another way of showing you regard the question as worthwhile is by pausing to think prior to answering it.

You may also show a lack of respect for the questioner by talking down to him. Typically (though not always), this is a mistake made by interviewers, rather than interviewees. Phrases such as "this may be hard for you to understand," "I used to think the same thing when I was your age," or "you may not believe me, but you will find out eventually" denigrate the questioner. An interviewee may make this mistake, too, by using phrases such as "as I've said before," or "as I thought I indicated on my resume." Finally, using profane language or language that the questioner should not be expected to understand—either because it is too technical or too hip—also shows disrespect.

3. *Answer questions honestly and directly.* Every interviewer and interviewee wants to deal with somebody he can trust. Answering questions honestly and directly shows the other person that he can trust you.

Interviewers or interviewees who waffle in response to uncomfortable questions hurt their causes. An honest and direct answer, on the other hand, is extremely disarming and, because it is relatively rare, is very effective.

For example, imagine two interviewees each of whom is asked whether he has ever produced an unsatisfactory work product. One interviewee responds as follows:

> "Well, not really. I mean I guess sometimes I am more satisfied with my work product than others. There may have been a few times when I wasn't really given a sufficient amount of time to polish up one of

my jobs quite as much as I would like to. But I'd say that is pretty rare. Usually, I do my best."

The other interviewee answers as follows:

"Yes. Summer before last I worked at XYZ Corporation. One of the vice-presidents asked me to write a memo on how we might attract a new client in the cosmetics industry. She really ripped my memo apart. She showed me how I should have organized it, pointed out approaches I should have considered, and stressed how I needed to support each of my conclusions. I redid the memo and the company used my revised memo as a basis to pitch the new client. Unfortunately, we didn't get the business. I felt pretty down when I got the criticism, but at the end of the summer I went back in to thank the person who criticized me."

Which answer do you think is more likely to impress the interviewer?

4. *Organize your answer.*   Flitting about from point to point, going forward, backward, and every which way in answering a question suggests that you would do the same thing on the job. Do not be afraid to take a little time before plunging into your answer. Consider ways to give your answer structure, either by organizing your response chronologically, organizing your points in order of their importance, or simply by starting your answer with a statement such as, "There are three things I would consider in answering that question. First . . ."

5. *Make your answers consistent with other answers you have given and with other behavior you have exhibited in the interview.*   For example, if you have told an employer you are a hard worker, then asking a bar-

rage of questions about whether you will have to work evenings, whether there is weekend work, and the length of vacations offered by the company will call into question your earlier self-assessment. Inconsistency on even one unimportant point may lead the other person to question the reliability of everything you have said in the interview.

6. *Do not run on at too great a length in response to a question.* An interview is supposed to be a dialogue, not a monologue. Neither interviewers nor interviewees appreciate an interview in which the other does almost all of the talking. Running on and on (and on) is a breach of the unwritten rules of interview etiquette.

   If you think you might be going on too long, cut your answer short. If the other person wants more information, he can always ask a follow-up question. Experienced interviewers and interviewees can gauge whether their answer is going on too long simply by watching the other person's reaction. A bored, expressionless look on the other's face, or shifting eyes, is a tip off that you are running on too long.

7. *Deliver your answers in a way that demonstrates you are interested in them and shows some energy on your part.* Often, this interest or energy is shown in your tone of voice or body language. Few things are worse than listening to an interviewer or interviewee drone on in response to a question in a monotone with an expression on her face that shows she would rather be almost any place other than where she is now. If *you* are not interested in or energized by your response, how can you expect the other person to be?

8. *Make sure your answer is credible and candid.* This

is not a repeat of guideline number three because an answer can be honest, but not credible. For example, consider an interviewer who, in response to being asked what he would change about his job replies, "No, there's not a single thing I can think of right now." Later, it turns out he has just begun his present position today. The initial reply is honest, but (without the explanation) not credible.

Don't memorize specific answers to questions you anticipate. Your answers will sound rehearsed and will lack spontaneity and credibility. For example, one "expert" on interviewing suggests in his book that interviewees answer the question, "What do you look for in a job?" as follows: "Personal fulfillment, consistent with effective administration." Anybody who gave me that stilted and phony answer would be out on his ear quickly.

9. *Make your answer interesting to the other party.* Of course, to do that, you need some sense of what the other person will be interested in. Using appropriate stories to illustrate your answer will help to make that answer both interesting and credible. It also helps to be aware of, and avoid, the clichès that have evolved and are used by both sides of the table in the interview process. These clichès vary from industry to industry and, within an industry, from year to year. For example, in law firms, the clichè of the year has moved from "collegial atmosphere" to "cutting edge work" to "quality of life." Be sensitive to the clichè of the year in your industry—and avoid using it.

10. *Answer in a way that shows you understand not only the question, but also the other person's reason for asking the question.* For example, the interviewee who asks about whether long hours are required

on the job, may well not be interested in knowing whether she will be able to leave at five-thirty, six, or six-thirty on an average night. More likely, she is interested in knowing whether she will have any life outside of work at all. Therefore, a response that said, "Yes, we work rather hard here, but we also have time for ourselves. For example, I am an avid skeet shooter, and I rarely miss one of our Wednesday evening or Saturday afternoon skeet-shooting club meetings," is far more responsive to the interviewee's concern than would be a reply such as, "On average, we work nineteen hundred hours per year." If you're in doubt about the reason for a question, ask the other person specifically why he asked it.

Of course, the substance of your answer counts. But, as the above guidelines suggest, the manner and form you use to convey your answer will determine how the other party responds to you. Put another way, you may say all the right things, but if you do not convey them with respect, credibility, directness, clarity, interest, conciseness, and understanding, you are unlikely to accomplish your purposes in the interview.

TEN

SELLING YOURSELF OR YOUR COMPANY

In addition to exchanging information, both parties want to use the interview to sell—the interviewee selling his qualifications and the interviewer the company and the job. In teaching people how to sell in the context of a job interview, I often encounter resistance. It's as if selling in this context is somehow dirty, or beneath both parties. Interviewers and interviewees both need to jettison that notion. There's nothing wrong with selling. Selling properly is not playing a game. Quite the opposite, in fact; selling means communicating in a way the other person understands.

You won't get the candidate (or job) you're looking for without selling. So as long as you must sell, you might just as well do it effectively. And honestly.

Some companies conduct a series of interviews with candidates and divide those interviews into evaluative and sell interviews, assuming that you can't do both in one interview. That's nonsense. Not only can you do them in one interview, you can be doing them at the same time within that interview. One of the biggest mistakes an interviewer makes in trying to sell candidates is to think he can sell only when he is talking. Think back on the last time you acquired something significant—a car, a house, a job. Did you acquire it because somebody talked at you constantly for a long time, or were other factors at least as important, such as how the person related to you or answered your questions (or whether you wanted the car or house in the first place).

Remember that you want to sell not only the star candidate you wish to hire, but also her roommate who may influence her decision, and other interviewees who will affect your reputation on campuses and in the marketplace and who may turn out to be your future customers, colleagues in the industry, or employees down the road. Of course, you will focus your selling efforts most strongly on candidates you've determined you want to hire, but don't ignore the techniques discussed in this chapter when interviewing candidates you will not extend offers to.

Though this chapter is written primarily from the employer's point of view, I have also included selling suggestions for the interviewee. As in most aspects of interviewing, the same principles apply to both sides of the table.

Indirect Selling in Screening Interviews

Especially in screening interviews, much of the selling that goes on from the interviewer's standpoint is indirect selling—the interviewer selling himself. In choosing a company in which they think they will feel comfortable, candidates judge their comfort level primarily from the way they react to the interviewers they meet. Indeed, to a student interviewing on campus, the interviewer *is* the company. Employers who find that notion a somewhat sobering thought may want to reconsider who they send as interviewers.

To a large extent, we've been talking about indirect selling all along in this book. Conducting a good interview sells. Therefore all of the elements that go into making a good interview—being prepared, being courteous and sensitive to the other person's feelings, and showing interest in the other party as a person—also help to sell.

And selling indirectly may have long-term impact. Here is the way one interviewee I spoke to almost twenty years ago described our interview:

> "Late in the fall of 1976 I went to a motel room in Cambridge, Massachusetts, to see a man I had never met. He was small and balding and wore a bow tie, and he spent most of the time we were together on the telephone, trying to comfort a client by explaining that the person who had been left in charge of the client's affairs was exceptionally able and had, in fact, just been made a partner. The man on the phone was Arnold B. Kanter, hiring partner at a prominent Chicago law firm; I was a second-year law student at Harvard, come to check on a possible summer job for which the weekly salary would exceed by half what I had made in my last term as a college teacher, the work I had done before going to law school.
>
> "When Arnie put down the phone I found him so cheerfully direct about the vagaries of the hiring process and the difficulty of being charming to thirty-some different law students over the course of two days in a warm hotel room that I confessed what I might not have—I was not all that serious about the job Arnie might have had available. My own anxieties with the summer-job scene had led me to make commitments—mental ones at least—about my plans. Nevertheless, I could not resist showing up to introduce myself. Arnie's firm was one of Chicago's powerhouses, and like most law students, I was confused enough about the future that I wanted to keep all options open. Arnie and I resolved to stay in touch; we had lunch over the summer, but we never did any of the further steps of the hiring waltz."

Despite the fact that we did not complete the waltz, some twelve years after our interview, the interviewee joined the law firm where I was a partner. His name is Scott Turow.

Casual Encounters

If your initial interviewers have done an effective job of screening, most candidates invited back for further interviews at your company should receive offers. Therefore, each interviewer at the company should start with the presumption that each interviewee he sees will be extended an offer.

Once a candidate is invited to a company, selling becomes a team effort by everyone at the company (whether they realize it or not). Interviewees notice how they are greeted by the receptionist, and whether their visit is expected. The respect, politeness, and good nature with which people treat one another in the hall and in their offices may have a substantial impact, consciously or subconsciously, on an interviewee's decision. This intangible is part of what candidates consider the "atmosphere" at a company. So every contact an interviewee has with anyone at the company becomes a potential selling (or alienating) opportunity.

If you are interviewing a candidate at your company, pay attention to where the next person the interviewee will be seeing is located. I remember consulting for a large Boston law firm. As I completed an interview with a partner there, he said to me, "Let's see, you're supposed to talk with Sally Smith next. Let me give her a call and find out where her office is."

He called Sally, asked where her office was and a sheepish grin came over his face as he hung up. Sally's office was two doors down from his. Had I been an interviewee seeking a position with the firm, that incident would have dissuaded me from accepting an offer.

Also, if you haven't met the next interviewer, take the time to do so before you bring the interviewee in. I have heard of times when a person from the company introduced himself to another person from the company, thinking that person was the interviewee. Even if you do not have enough time to meet the person before you bring the interviewee in, you can avoid being mistaken for the interviewee by introducing the real interviewee to the next interviewer quickly as you enter the office.

Besides avoiding an embarrassing situation, there is another reason to know who the next interviewer is. If you do, you will have an opportunity to talk that interviewer up to the interviewee by saying something positive about her. This simple effort gives the interviewee a favorable impression of camaraderie within the company. If the interviewer does not initiate this type of discussion, the interviewee may do so and in that way use the walk between interviews to learn something about his next interviewer.

Unplanned, casual encounters can have an impact on your ability to attract a candidate. One hiring partner friend of mine tells of the time he was interviewing at a prestigious law firm in Chicago. Between interviews, he asked if he could stop in the men's room.

The person taking him to the next interview showed him into the men's room and waited there for him, by the sink, as my friend disappeared to attend to business. A few seconds later another lawyer from the firm came into the men's room and, seeing the fellow by the sink holding a resume, asked if he could take a look at it. He perused the resume for several seconds and then announced, "Nothing spectacular," handing him back the resume, just as my friend reappeared in the sink area.

Recognizing his gaff, the lawyer who had asked to see the

resume tried to cover by introducing himself enthusiastically saying, "Hi, I'm Bob Jones."

My friend shook his hand saying, "Hi, Bob, I'm nothing spectacular."

Turned out that the law firm *did* think he was spectacular, and extended him an offer. My friend did not accept.

An interviewee should also recognize that every contact he has with a company is a potential selling (or alienating) opportunity. Your resume, your cover letter, the way you treat people in the personnel office or interviewers' secretaries, how you handle a dinner, lunch, or other entertainment with people from the company, the discretion you use in submitting expenses for reimbursement may all have a direct bearing on how you are evaluated by the company.

Though it's fine to distinguish yourself in your cover letter, there is a limit to how creative you should be. One candidate sent the following letter to a prominent Los Angeles law firm:

Dear Sirs:

I realize that you probably receive at least two or three unsolicited resumes per week. I must, therefore, impress upon you that this particular unsolicited resume is worthy of special consideration. With that in mind, I respectfully request that you sing the remainder of this cover letter to the tune of "My Bonnie Lies Over the Ocean."

When your firm requires new lawyers,
must they have a Harvard degree?
Is law review taken for granted?
Or would you choose someone like me?

Pick me
Pick me
My zeal to work for you is true (is true).
What more, What more
To prove it what more could I do?

Top notch is my research and writing.
Assignments delivered on time.
I know what you're thinking, don't worry.
Not all of my work product rhymes.

Choose me
Choose me
You'll find I'm the one for the job (the job).
At least, I have
distinguished myself from the mob.

A resume comes with these lyrics.
Included for you to peruse.
Perhaps I've been too informal.
I really have nothing to lose.

Call me
Call me
In person we really should speak (should speak)
Thank you, Thank you
I'll contact you sometime next week.

Sincerely,

The letter did not have its intended effect. And I don't recommend singing your answers in an interview to the tune of "Clementine," either.

Direct Selling

Effective direct selling in an interview involves three steps: (a) identifying what the "buyer" wants, (b) identifying what your company has that meets those desires, and (c) communicating effectively what you have to offer the candidate.

Determine what a candidate wants by listening and observing, and by asking directly. Listening is on-the-spot market research for you. And listening in itself sells because it shows interest in the interviewee. In any case, selling before you determine what the candidate is looking for is approaching the process backward. Touting virtues the interviewee has no interest in is at best a waste of time and, at worst, counterproductive.

An interviewer must know the company well in order to respond with what you have to offer a candidate. Of course, there's no substitute for experience in teaching interviewers what your company has to offer. At a minimum, each interviewer should review all of the material a candidate is likely to have seen. If an interviewer has doubts about how to handle certain questions or situations, he should speak to the person in charge of your recruitment efforts.

Some companies spend considerable time trying to figure out what characteristics of the company they should be selling to candidates. Though that is putting the cart somewhat before the horse, it is still a useful exercise. Make sure that you focus on selling a limited number of characteristics, though. Pretending to be everything to candidates simply is not credible.

Effective communication means speaking in language the interviewee can both understand and relate to. For example the law-student candidate who says he is interested in challenging legal work is unlikely to respond to your comment that you just handled a fascinating 378(q)8(ii) exchange involving a sale-leaseback with a wrap mortgage backed by a Eurodollar loan. Law (like most other businesses today) is extremely complicated. Many entry-level candidates will not have a full appreciation of those complications. For that reason, you must make sure you describe characteristics of your company in a way candidates can understand.

Assume you will be struck dead upon the spot if you use more than one of the following phrases during any single interview:

cutting edge
sophisticated
collegial
diversity
early responsibility

These catchphrases are used frequently in investment banks and law firms; others may apply in your industry. The point is to avoid using the types of hackneyed phrases that are calculated to cause interviewees' eyes to glaze over because they hear them from every employer with whom they interview. Find new, fresher ways of expressing what you are trying to get across. Use your own words, instead of the buzzwords of the day. An interviewee is more likely to relate favorably to an interviewer who tells her about the "incredibly mind-boggling deal" he just worked on than she is to one who speaks of the "cutting-edge nature of the project" he just completed.

Not surprisingly, the same principles that help an interviewer to sell effectively will help the interviewee as well. He, too, must understand what the "buyer" wants, identify what he has that fulfills those needs, and communicate in a language that the interviewer can understand (and relate to).

The language problem from an interviewee's standpoint is unlikely to be the use of technical terms the interviewer cannot understand. Rather, some interviewees lapse into the latest lingo, which often does considerable violence to the English language. I can attest to the grating sound of an interviewee who says, "so, I'm like," when he means, "then I said," or "that would be like rilly cool," when she means "I would like that." Apart from the other problems this language creates, it accentuates the generation gap between an interviewee and an interviewer, making the latter feel older than he might like to consider himself. That's probably not something an interviewee ought to do.

Benefits and Features

In the end, each candidate wants to know "What's in it for me?" Therefore, you should concentrate on selling the *benefits* of your company, rather than its *features*. "Benefits" are what something means to a candidate. "Features" are merely descriptive. Part of your job in selling is to convert features into benefits. To give you an idea of how to do that, listed below are examples of some common features of companies, followed by corresponding benefits to candidates:

1. *A young company*—opportunity for growth, ability for you to relate to other employees.
2. *Major customers/clients*—interesting work you'd do, stability.
3. *Support services*—you can focus on the job you've been hired to do, on interesting work.
4. *Excellent employees*—you will be trained by the best, opportunity to observe them in action.
5. *Pleasant people*—the time you spend at the company will be enjoyable.
6. *Cutting-edge work*—you will be challenged and stimulated.
7. *Lack of structure*—you will not be inhibited in your growth by a lot of rules and formalities.
8. *Small office/break down into groups*—you will not be lost, you will be a valued member of the team.
9. *Prestige of the company*—you will feel proud to work here, you are not limiting your future options.

10. *Well-managed*—you are coming into a stable, successful company, you won't have to worry about things other than doing your job well.

Notice that all of the benefits speak in terms of "you," the interviewee. Interviewers should begin to make interviewees feel they are part of the company by conveying to them, "This is what it would be like if you were working with us." The best way of selling anything is to make the buyer feel he owns it. People love to buy once they own something.

Like the interviewer, the interviewee, too, can improve her selling efforts by understanding the difference between features and benefits. Convert your selling points into benefits to the employer. For example, assume that the job you are interviewing for requires you to put out a monthly client newsletter. Instead of simply referring to your attention to detail, you might say, "You could be comfortable that I would not let that newsletter be sent out to clients without double-checking to make sure there were no errors in it." This type of statement not only identifies the benefit to the employer, but also shows that you are focused on getting specific tasks done, an important characteristic for most any employee.

Specifics versus Generalities

Wherever possible, sell with specifics, not generalities. Candidates are numb to platitudinous claims of significant responsibility early on, an excellent training program, and fine prospects for advancement. So instead of talking about your excellent training program, pull out a copy of the training schedule for the next month and review it with the candidate.

Interviewers who point to personal experiences are especially effective. For example, instead of talking about how rewarding work at your company is, in general, talk about the time you . . . and how you felt about accomplishing that. This will humanize you to the interviewee, and help to lend credibility to what you say. (Of course you'll want to avoid lapsing into a series of war stories that consume the entire interview.)

In conducting interviews at companies to help them identify what they should be selling to candidates, I often ask those I'm interviewing what they think the company should be selling. I generally get a reply from a young employee that goes something like, "I think we should be selling the early responsibility new people get." Typically this is said in a flat tone with no discernible interest or conviction.

But if I then ask the person what she did yesterday, it is as if I am speaking to a different person. Her eyes light up, she smiles, her voice is alive, she is energetic, often picking things up or pointing to them. All of this animation occurs because she is talking about something real that interests her, rather than an abstraction. Which do you think is more effective in selling an interviewee?

Where appropriate, use statistics or specific examples. For example, compare the different effect on an interviewee of a company representative talking about "the great diversity of people at the company" and one who points to "employees in the division you would be joining attended twenty-six colleges and twenty of them hold advanced degrees, outside their initial majors."

For interviewees, it's extremely important to speak in terms of specific, personal experiences, rather than generalities. Employers are unlikely to be impressed by blanket statements such as "I'm a resourceful person."

But try telling them about the time you had to have

something photocopied at midnight in order to deliver it to a client waiting up for it at her home, and the copy machine broke down after thirty pages of a seventy-page document. The local photocopy store was closed for the night. You remembered, though, that a friend of yours knew one of the people who worked at the photocopy store. You called your friend, explained the situation, and convinced him to call his friend to open the store. In the meantime, you delivered the first thirty pages to the client, and told her you'd bring the rest within the hour. You rushed back to the photocopy store, picked up the remaining pages and got them into the hands of your client, who was reading page twenty-seven at the time. The next day, you sent boxes of candy and a note to your friend and the person who opened the photocopy store. You asked your friend for the home phone number of his friend at the store, and put that number in your phone book for future reference. Now *that's* a resourceful person.

Visual aids can be useful for an interviewer. Don't be afraid to pull down a book from a bookshelf, point to a picture on the wall, refer to the telephone messages on your desk, walk over to the window to show the interviewee some of the buildings your clients or customers are located in, or open to the company telephone directory to show an interviewee the extent of your support staff. These things will make your point come alive.

Visual aids will be more difficult for an interviewee to use, because pulling objects out of a briefcase during an interview is bound to appear staged. In some circumstances, though, it may be appropriate for you to draw a diagram or map to explain something you are talking about to the interviewer.

Dealing with the Competition

Most of the candidates you recruit will have offers from other excellent companies. Focus on selling your company, not on tearing down others. Bad-mouthing other companies is always counterproductive in the long run, even if you regard them as a distinctly inferior choice to yours. For one thing, by disparaging another company, you are disparaging the interviewee who has told you he is seriously considering accepting an offer with that company. Indeed, you should use the interview to learn what candidates find attractive about your competitors. It may be that you have something similar (or better) to offer, or that you should develop something comparable.

Of course, there is no reason not to point out factual differences between your company and competitors. In many cases, these differences will be neutral—some interviewees may prefer one and others another. Naturally, you will try to highlight factual differences you believe will appeal to the interviewee. Just make sure your facts are right. Making a false statement about a competitor will call into question the veracity of everything you've said to the interviewee.

Stories, Trying Something Different, and Enthusiasm

Where appropriate, communicate by telling stories. People listening to a story are less skeptical, more inclined to accept what you are saying. And people remember stories. Telling a story is also an excellent way of establishing rapport with the other person. Make your story short, though. And be sure it has a point.

My friend, Syd Lieberman, who is a professional storyteller, tells the tale of Yankel, the fool. One day Yankel was working in the field when a man rode by on horseback and noticed that painted on Yankel's barn were twelve targets, each with a tiny bull's-eye. There was an arrow in the exact center of each bull's-eye. The man stopped and called to Yankel, "Yankel, who shot these arrows?"

"I shot them, but why do you ask?" replied Yankel.

"Because you must be the greatest marksman in all the world, hitting the center of each of these bull's-eyes."

"Ah," said Yankel, "I am afraid that you are mistaken, I am not much of a marksman."

"But these bull's-eyes, the arrows?"

"Yes, but you see first I shoot the arrows, then I paint the bull's-eyes."

So gather a quiver-full of your story-arrows in advance, and shoot them into the bull's-eyes when you see them.

Don't be afraid to try something different in an interview. I recall the time I was interviewing a woman who, prior to going to law school, had spent some time ghostwriting a book for a man in a small town in Indiana. It seems this fellow had made a pile of dough auctioning off the contents of hotels that had gone bankrupt, and wanted his exploits to be immortalized in a book.

I asked the interviewee whether she still maintained contact with the hotel auctioneer. She said no, she hadn't spoken to him in about three years. "So let's call him," I suggested.

After she picked herself off the floor, she responded, "But we can't do that. I don't know his phone number."

"Well, he lives in this little town in Indiana, doesn't he? Let's just call information," I said.

We called information, got his phone number and the fellow happened to be in. I put him on the speaker phone and the interviewee and I had a pleasant, ten-minute conversation with her former employer.

As I recall, we were not successful in hiring the interviewee (she went to a New York firm), but I'll bet anything she remembers our interview. Being memorable in a positive way is a good goal for an interviewer to establish in trying to sell a candidate.

Finally, genuine enthusiasm is catching. An interviewer or interviewee who sells with enthusiasm is far more likely to convince than the person who appears to be giving a pat response for the fiftieth time (even if the response is in fact true and it is the fiftieth time the person has given it). The depth of your conviction, not the height of your logic, is what sells. As one interviewee put it, "Nothing turned me off faster than the interviewers who sounded as if they'd rather be hauling trash than talking to me, or who sounded bored with their lives."

Producing a Commercial

In teaching interviewers how to sell their company more effectively, I sometimes put them through an exercise. I ask them to imagine they are preparing a thirty-second television commercial selling their company to interviewees. (Interviewees, of course, may do the same thing, imagining that they are selling themselves to an employer.) After they have prepared the commercial, I ask them to perform it. From my observations, ten qualities tend to emerge in these commercials:

1. They are extremely visual.
2. They are personal.
3. They are creative and engaging.
4. They are simple and use easily understandable language.
5. They tell a story.
6. They speak about human concerns.
7. They are positive, upbeat and enthusiastic.

8. They are directed at the interests of the people at whom they are aimed.
9. They are short.
10. They have a theme.

Interviewers and interviewees would both do well to keep these ten qualities in mind in trying to sell themselves.

Entertainment

Until now, we have assumed that all of the interviews would take place either on campus or at the company's office. But a company may also decide to conduct interviews over lunch or dinner. That setting may prove an excellent opportunity to sell a candidate, and may also give both parties a useful forum to explore more personal elements of their decisions.

One initial caution here, prompted by the reference to "personal elements." The informal setting is fertile ground for trouble in the area of discriminatory hiring practices. You should not say anything over an interview lunch or dinner that you would not say in your office. Nor, of course, should this interview meal become the setting for starting a romance.

When you take an interviewee out to lunch, choose a comfortable and quiet restaurant, one that affords an opportunity for relaxed discussion. Your goal should not be to take him to the most expensive restaurant in town, but to select one that is either unusual or typical of your city. Your company may want to develop a list of suggested eating places and update it from time to time.

Not more than two others, generally people not much above the candidate's level, should accompany an interviewee for lunch to avoid overwhelming him. The objectives of the interview lunch should be to provide an informal opportunity for the interviewee to relate to people at the company and to afford the company an opportunity to observe and evaluate the interviewee in a social setting. An interviewee who abuses the waiter or wine steward is unlikely to deal sensitively with customers or clients.

Though you may choose to make your interview dinner somewhat more elaborate than lunch, the same basic principles apply. Generally not more than two people should take an interviewee out to dinner. If the interviewee has a spouse or significant other, you may want to include couples in your dinner plans. Stopping by an employee's house before dinner for a drink and hors d'oeuvres will give an interviewee a chance to see how people at your company live, and lends a more personal flavor to the evening. That should prove effective in selling your company.

Though lunch or dinner provides a more relaxed setting, interviewees should make no mistake—that lunch or dinner is an interview.

ELEVEN

IDENTIFYING AND HANDLING OBSTACLES

Successful recruitment or job hunting involves more than touting your virtues. Identifying and handling problems—the obstacles you face in recruitment—is no less important. No company or interviewee is perfect so it is best not to pretend you are. Indeed, dealing with obstacles in a forthright manner can be an effective selling tool.

Identifying Obstacles

The obstacles an employer faces in recruitment will surface in the form of questions, comments, or concerns from interviewees. To identify those obstacles, you must establish a relationship with the candidate so that he feels free to mention his concerns. (The same holds true for the interviewee.) This will be much easier to accomplish later in the interview, after you have demonstrated your interest in the interviewee.

You may draw the candidate out directly by asking him

his concerns in choosing a company in general (the things he mentions will likely be concerns he has with your company) or by asking him specifically what concerns he has about your company. Some interviewees will be more comfortable if you ask them what concerns *others* have expressed about your company, so they do not have to acknowledge that it is their concern, as well.

In some instances, you may not wait for an interviewee to raise a concern. For example, if a particular concern has surfaced repeatedly among students at a given school, you may decide to broach the concern with other students from the school. Raising the matter yourself may impress the interviewee with your candor, and make her feel more comfortable in raising other concerns. Generally, your company's reputation spreads quickly around a school so there is relatively little risk that other students will not have heard it. The same may not be as true between schools so you should be more careful raising a concern expressed, for example, by several Michigan students with a student from Harvard. You could be unnecessarily raising doubts in a student's mind.

Your company should compile a list of specific obstacles candidates have raised. Each interviewer should be prepared to respond to each obstacle. These should not be memorized answers, of course, nor should everybody at the company have the same response. As with your selling points, you should review the obstacles you encounter annually. They are likely to change from year to year. And even if they don't, you may come up with more effective ways of dealing with them.

CATEGORIES OF OBSTACLES

A candidate's (or an interviewer's) concerns usually fall into one of four general categories:

1. *Misunderstandings*—you should acknowledge some responsibility for the misunderstanding, perhaps by saying that the company's description (or your resume) should have been clearer or that you should have made a point clearer. Then you should correct the misunderstanding, presenting facts whenever possible. An example might be an interviewee who has the impression she must choose a single department in which to work immediately when in fact your company encourages people to rotate between departments.

2. *Skepticism*—you should acknowledge the interviewee's concern, make him feel it is a legitimate concern, provide objective information to alleviate the concern and/or refer the question to another person, either within the company or outside, who can address the interviewee's skepticism. Another way to deal with skepticism is to suggest that the interviewee observe the situation himself; in effect, that he answer his own concern.

   For example, a minority candidate might be skeptical about the company's commitment to diversity. In response, you might point specifically to what the company is doing to promote diversity, cite the number of minorities hired recently, and invite the candidate to talk to minority employees at the company.

   People who have come to your company laterally from other employers will be particularly effective, both in selling your company to candidates and in dealing with obstacles you encounter. They have what the perspective candidates are searching for—the experience that allows them to compare one company with another. They also can assure a candidate that although they once had the same reservations the candidate has about your company, they have discov-

ered from experience that those concerns were not
well founded.

3. *Real drawbacks*—you should admit the drawback,
point to what you are doing to correct it, and encourage the interviewee to look at the bigger picture in
order to conclude that the drawback should not be
decisive. An example of a real drawback might be the
recent loss of a large customer or a key company
officer or the adoption of a government regulation
that adversely affects the company's business.

4. *Obstacles that should not be overcome*—certain types
of concerns of an interviewee may be so substantially
at odds with what your company has to offer that
you should not attempt to counteract them. In these
relatively rare circumstances, you will do the interviewee and ultimately your company a favor by
acknowledging the fact and accepting that the interviewee may be happier someplace else.

Principles for Dealing with Obstacles

Once you understand the type of obstacle you are dealing
with, certain general principles should help you deal with
the tough questions or concerns you face. Here are fifteen
principles for both interviewers and interviewees (note that
some are the same as those used for effective selling because
dealing with obstacles is the flip side of selling, and others
are similar to the principles for answering questions because
many obstacles appear as questions):

1. *Establish a relationship with the other person before
inviting questions.* You will accomplish that by
showing real interest in the other person. Until you
have established that relationship no answer you give
will have much credibility.

2. *If you don't know the answer to a question, say so, and get back to the other person.* Faking an answer is a big mistake. The person may well find out later what the correct answer is, which will call into question everything you have said during the interview. By the way, getting back to somebody with an answer is an excellent selling opportunity because so few people do it.

3. *Acknowledge the legitimacy of the other person's concerns.* You may do that simply by treating the question seriously and answering it, or you may use such comments as "That's a good question," "I can understand why you would be concerned about that," or "Yes, I've heard that from other interviewees." Everybody likes to feel his concerns are legitimate. Unless you acknowledge this, the person may not be listening to your answer.

4. *Where problems exist, acknowledge them.* If you admit even one problem ("Yes, we're sometimes not as good about giving people positive feedback as we should be."), that will lend credibility to whatever else you say in the interview. At the same time, of course, you should point out any progress you have made in solving the problem, or any steps you are taking to address it.

5. *Be honest, but don't shoot yourself in the foot.* As an interviewer you cannot hope to learn as much about the interviewee as he knows about himself. Your company is *not* the right one for every candidate, and you must rely, in part, on the interviewee to make that assessment for himself. (Likewise, the candidate cannot hope to know the job or the company fully and so must rely on the interviewer.) For that reason, you want to provide not only a favorable

impression of your company, but also a realistic and honest one.

There is a big difference, though, between being candid and gratuitously knocking yourself or your company. For example, it is appropriate to answer an interviewee's question about turnover in the company, but you would not want to begin the interview by reciting how many people have left the company in the past year.

6. *Answer relatively briefly.* If, in response to a touchy question, you run on at great length, the substance of what you say will not make much difference. You will have protested too much. The length of your answer will convince the other person that a significant problem exists.

7. *Don't argue with the other party.* You may win the argument, but lose the job (or the candidate).

8. *Use specific facts or examples, where possible.* A woman who expresses concern about the company's attitude toward employees who have children would be more impressed to know that four senior officers of the company raised families while continuing to work at the company, five women are currently on six-month maternity leave, and eight women are working part-time than she would be to hear that "the company is very supportive of family values." These facts or examples will make your answer more credible to the other person.

9. *Speak about your personal experience.* If the interviewee is concerned about being pigeonholed in a small area of the company, tell him how you moved from engineering to sales to corporate development. This approach will add credibility to your answer.

10. *Have people at the appropriate levels address problems*

that are raised. A senior officer cannot speak credibly about morale among junior people at the company, nor can a junior person speak convincingly of promotional opportunities or the company's long-term strategic plan.

11. *Explain the basis for the obstacle, but don't become too defensive.* For example, an interviewee who is asked about how she happened to choose to attend a second-tier business school might reply, "I was offered a full scholarship at X University, and I couldn't be more pleased with the quality of the education I feel I am getting."

12. *Address the concern that is raised.* First, you must make sure that you understand the other person's concern. Where there is doubt, it is perfectly appropriate to clarify the nature of the concern.

   For example, in interviewer-training sessions I have heard many interviewers respond at great length to a concern expressed by an interviewee that the firm has a reputation as a sweatshop. The classic definition of a sweatshop is a place in which people work extremely long hours doing dull, repetitive work for low wages in unpleasant working conditions for abusive people. Which aspects of this definition does an interviewee have in mind?

   If you don't know, your response may well be off target and may even raise problems in the interviewee's mind that did not exist before. In this circumstance, an interviewer should consider a response such as the following, "You know, I've heard that before and I'm concerned about it. Before I respond, though, I'm curious to know what you mean when you say 'sweatshop.' "

13. *Beware of unwittingly reinforcing your company's reputation.* An interviewee will be looking to con-

firm the negative aspects of that reputation and may find confirmation in your interview style or in little things she observes during the course of a day of interviews. For example, a stress interview will confirm a company's reputation as a tough place to work. Similarly, a company known to be internally competitive will reinforce that reputation if one department knocks the capability of those in another department, even if it is done in jest.

14. *Do not joke about problems.* If the interviewee asks whether there is time outside of work to pursue other interests, don't say, "Sure, I saw my wife, ah . . . Harriet, that's it, just a few weeks ago." The interviewee may assume you are making light of her concern or of the problem, or both. The interviewee would not raise the concern if she thought it was funny.

15. *Emphasize the positive.* Once you've answered the person's concern directly, honestly, and briefly, point out the positive aspects of any concern. For example, an interviewer who is responding to an interviewee's concern about the long hours required of employees might say, "Yes, we do have to work long hours from time to time, but that's because the challenging nature of our work demands it. When everyone is caught up in the excitement of a transaction, nobody seems to mind being down here to do what needs to be done. And there are peaks and valleys, so we are not working long hours all of the time."

Sensitivity to Language

In dealing with obstacles, it's important to recognize the importance of the words you choose. Exactly the same characteristics may be described in vastly different ways. Here are some common phrases interviewees use to describe characteristics of companies and possible "translations" for them. The characteristics in the left-hand column are (or may be considered) negative; those on the right are generally more positive.

Characteristic	Translation
sink or swim	on the job training, early responsibility
sweatshop	busy, hardworking, successful, demanding
competitive	open, opportunity, meritocracy
disorganized	flexible, nonhierarchical, democratic, individualistic, creative
large	stable, successful, diverse
aggressive	innovative, motivated, dynamic
arrogant	proud, confident, successful
turnover	training, opportunity, mobility
pushed	challenged

Characteristic	*Translation*
aloof	professional
conservative	civil, polite

Being familiar with these "translations" should help interviewers govern their own choice of words with interviewees and deal more effectively with interviewees' concerns. For example, an interviewer probably should not use the phrase "sink or swim" himself. And faced with a comment by an interviewee that she's heard the company was a "sink or swim" type place, an interviewer might reply, "well, we do give people a lot of responsibilities early on. We believe the best way to learn, though, is through on-the-job training. Of course, some people do not work out; but that happens in any company."

Interviewees should recognize these translations, as well. It will help you become aware that there often is more than one way to look at a company's characteristics. In addition, it may shed light on how you (and others) view your own strengths and weaknesses. Indeed, some of the translations above may apply to your own characteristics: disorganized, aggressive, and arrogant, for example.

In addition to these translations, you should be sensitive to the impact of other choices of language, as well. A poor word choice can turn a harmless comment into a disaster, and vice versa. I recall a mock interview in which the interviewee asked the interviewer about turnover at the company. The interviewer started her reply with, "When I lose my friends . . ." She then made a good, positive statement about how these people went on to excellent positions. However, what stuck in my mind (and the mock interviewee confirmed that it stuck in hers, too) was the image of "losing friends," which both of us imagined as deaths.

Conversely, in another mock interview, the interviewer was asked a difficult question about how it was to work in a relatively small outpost of a large New York company. She said, "It's great, I view the people in our New York office as distant cousins, they're there to help when you need them." In one fell swoop she converted a difficult question about a large, impersonal-sounding company into a family gathering.

TWELVE

CLOSING THE INTERVIEW

You have made it through twenty minutes of a thirty-minute screening interview. Congratulations. You are starting to worry about ending this thing. You think it is time to close the interview. You are wrong.

If you start to close the interview now, you will deprive yourself of valuable time you could use to learn more about the interviewee. Let's assume your opening took three minutes. That means you've spent only seventeen minutes learning about the interviewee, so far. Take another five minutes to learn more. That may not seem like much time, but think of it this way—if you use that extra five minutes to learn about the interviewee, you will have acquired almost thirty percent additional information about the candidate. That's significant.

You should, however, save five minutes to conclude a screening interview. How should you use that five minutes?

1. Thank the interviewee for taking time to interview with your company.
2. Explain when and how the interviewee will hear from you about possible follow-up interviews.
3. Invite questions from the candidate. In general, the type of questions you want to encourage in an initial interview are questions that would affect the candidate's decision as to whether to participate in further interviews with the company. You don't want the candidate to trot out a list of twenty questions she has memorized, but does not care a whit about the answers to. If you are having trouble drawing out a candidate's questions or concerns, ask whether she is "curious about anything" at your company. This phrasing will make the interviewee feel freer to raise concerns because they are "curiosities," rather than direct challenges.
4. You may also ask the interviewee, "Is there anything we haven't covered that we should have?" Not only may this elicit useful information, it also has the advantage of giving the interviewee a final opportunity to make a favorable impression, whether or not he uses it.
5. Any overt selling in a screening interview should generally be done during the closing five minutes of the interview, typically in response to the interviewee's questions.
6. If the interview has run the full time without an opportunity for questions (or even if there have been a few questions), you may invite the interviewee to phone you if he has (additional) questions. (This is an excellent opportunity for you to unload some of those hard-to-get-rid-of business cards.) Don't worry about being inundated by phone calls. Few interviewees will take you up on your offer.

7. Tell the interviewee you have enjoyed talking with her. If you really have, chances are you conducted a good interview.
8. Shake hands with the interviewee, and look him in the eye, as you say good-bye.
9. Walk the interviewee to the door.
10. Try to leave the interviewee with an up-beat impression of the company (and you).

As with the other interview "rules," the above are only guidelines. You should feel free to vary the format when special circumstances (or your instincts) tell you that would be desirable.

For an interviewee, there are only three important things to remember about the closing. (Though, of course, you, too, should thank the interviewer, telling him you've enjoyed talking to him and shake hands firmly, looking him in the eye.) If you do have questions about the company that would affect whether you would want to spend further time interviewing with it, make sure you get a chance to ask those questions during the interview. Also, if the interviewer has failed to elicit some important information about you, make sure you sneak it in before the interview ends. Finally, find out what the next step will be, and when it is likely to occur.

If you fail to accomplish those objectives, follow up with the interviewer once she returns to her office. Do that, though, only when you need to. Interviewers are not impressed by follow-up efforts that only attempt to get their ear or flaunt your word processing capabilities. That type of follow-up will be counterproductive.

THIRTEEN

ACHIEVING DIVERSITY AND AVOIDING DISCRIMINATORY QUESTIONS

Most books on interviewing begin and end their discussion of discriminatory questions by assessing the legality of an interviewer's behavior. To me, that's got it backward. Interviewers should start out with an appreciation of the need for, and value of, diversity. In recent years, many companies have begun to place real value on diversity in their workforce, and have seriously tried to achieve it.

Why Diversity?

Diverse means different from, unlike. It does not mean better or worse than, just different. Nor does diversity relate only to the color of one's skin or to one's sex, but also to differences in culture, values, customs, and mores. Unfortunately, many people have a tendency to be afraid of, threatened by, or put off by diversity.

As a personal example, I wear a bow tie. I often start out my interviewer training programs by asking participants, after only a minute or two, to write down three characteristics they think I possess. Here are twenty of the responses I've gotten:

liberal	confident
conservative	academic
weird	idiosyncratic
funny	prissy
brash	witty
offbeat	irreverent
thoughtful	stylish
courageous	serious
shy	antiauthoritarian
intellectual	impulsive

I could give you more, but the point is that what was different about me—something as innocuous as a bow tie— evoked strong (and often flatly contradictory) reactions from people who did not know me. How much more reaction, then, may differences in race, nationality, religion, and sex evoke?

Why should a company want diversity? For many reasons:

1. Different backgrounds may help you develop different (and, in some cases, better) approaches to solving your business problems. A homogeneous group of people will not bring the range of perspectives that may lead to the best solutions. Indeed, they may not even appreciate all aspects of the problem.
2. Diversity is a hedge against being wrong. Consider the securities industry, where mutual funds and diversified

investment portfolios contribute to arriving at an overall sound investment pool. Diversity in your workforce serves the same purpose.

3. The marketplace is increasingly composed of women and minorities. By the year 2000, they will constitute a majority of the workforce. Therefore, your company's ability to fill its personnel needs will *require* that you attract diverse people.

4. The people buying a company's products and services are themselves increasingly diverse. To achieve your business goals, it is important to understand how your customers and clients approach problems, and to be able to point to people like them in your company.

What Prevents Achieving Diversity?

Most of us think of ourselves as unbiased. And I assume that readers of this book would not intentionally discriminate. What, then, gets in the way of achieving diversity in your hiring efforts?

Let's recognize that conducting a good interview with somebody different from you requires some effort. Think back on some of the best interviews you've participated in. Chances are you hit it off with the other person because of some shared, common experience or background. Indeed, I have suggested that noting this type of common experience is a way to establish rapport with the interviewee, to get the interview off to a good, comfortable start. However, those shared, common experiences are less likely to occur between interviewers and interviewees who are of different colors, sexes, and nationalities from one another. To make matters worse, many of the common interview mistakes pointed to in this book, particularly in chapter 15, get in the way of achieving diversity. Consider the following:

If you conduct stress interviews, you will be contributing to an atmosphere that will be uncomfortable and may get in the way of establishing rapport with diverse people.

If you have not identified the true criteria for whom you should be hiring, you are more likely to apply discriminatory criteria.

If you are looking for drinking buddies, you will likely hire people who are similar to you.

If you are asking repetitive, routine questions, you will not allow diverse people to emerge in ways that may make them attractive to your company.

If you are looking for yourself in each interviewee, and you are not diverse, chances are you will not hire diverse people.

If you assume that somebody who looks the part can play the part, that part has probably traditionally been played by a white male.

If you think that Harvard and Yale graduates walk on water, you may demonstrate an elitism that rules out many minorities.

If you are looking for candidates who will "fit" into your company, unconsciously you may use that test to exclude diverse people.

If you are extremely conservative in your decision making, the safe choice may be the nondiverse choice.

In other words, playing the interview game gets in the way of diversity.

All of the above are serious obstacles to creating a diverse workforce in your company. A heightened awareness of and sensitivity to these obstacles should help you overcome them. Imagine that you were the minority or diverse person in the interview. Think about how you would feel; what might offend you, what might make you comfortable? Look for common ground with interviewees, not differences. Take a sincere interest in and show curiosity about interviewees. Look not only for numerical grade-point averages, but for potential, as well.

Illegal Questions

The obvious reason for avoiding discriminatory questions is that they are against the law, but you will also want to avoid them because they can adversely affect your company's reputation for many years. In egregious situations, schools may bar companies whose on-campus interviewers violate school policies against discrimination from interviewing on campus. Even when that does not occur, adverse publicity or bad word-of-mouth may have lasting effects on a company's recruitment efforts.

Rather than try to cover in detail what constitutes an illegal question, I have listed the principal federal statutes on the subject in the Appendix. (You must also take into account laws or ordinances that apply in your state or city.) Lest you think the problem of illegal questions is arcane, not a real problem anymore, opposite is the form that interviewers for a Texas *law firm* were asked to complete not too many years ago:

ATTORNEY/LAW CLERK INTERVIEW SHEET

RECOMMENDATION: (NEED PHOTOGRAPH/TRANSCRIPT)

Position Desired: Attorney/Law Clerk

NAME:

AGE: DATE AVAILABLE: TEXAS BAR EXAM:

DATE:

UNDERGRADUATE—GPA: CLASS RANKING:

LAW SCHOOL—GPA: CLASS RANKING:

1. Are you married? Spouse's Name:
2. Do you plan marriage soon? Fiancé(e)'s name:
3. Where did you grow up?
4. Where did your spouse/fiancé(e) grow up?
5. What does your spouse/fiancé(e) do?
6. Where do your parents live?
   (a) Mother
   (b) Father
7. Where do your spouse's/fiancé(e)'s parents live?
   (a) Mother
   (b) Father
8. What do your parents do for a living?
   (a) Mother
   (b) Father
9. What do your spouse's/fiancé(e)'s parents do for a living?
   (a) Mother
   (b) Father
10. How do you and your spouse/fiancé(e) feel about living and working in the area?

Some general, practical guidelines will help you to steer clear of trouble. One way of avoiding illegal questions is to focus on questions that are job-related. However, not all questions you may believe are job-related are necessarily nondiscriminatory. For example, some men may believe that asking a woman about her child-bearing plans is job-related because having a child may prevent her from working for a period of time, but federal law prohibits that question. Asking non-job-related questions, though, only heightens the chances that you will run afoul of nondiscrimination standards.

You needn't lapse into asking the old "worst question" syndrome in order to avoid illegal questions, though. Remember that a wide range of questions may be job-related—asking about an experience waiting tables, a college thesis, even butterfly collecting.

If you find yourself asking certain questions only of particular categories of interviewees—for example minorities, women, disabled—watch out. You should not ask questions of any category of interviewees that you would not ask all interviewees. If you find yourself starting a question with "I probably shouldn't be asking this, but . . ." don't ask the question.

Do not ask questions of candidates because you think your clients or customers may have certain prejudices. Let's assume, for example, that one of your major customers has told you he will cease doing business with you if you employ persons of a particular religion or nationality. This would not justify your refusing to hire a person of that religion or nationality, because client prejudices can never excuse your acting discriminatorily in your hiring.

Another way to steer clear of discriminatory practices is to avoid asking questions that make impermissible assumptions. For example, asking a woman about child care presumes (a) that it's a legitimate concern when a woman is being interviewed, but not when a man is; (b) that women always have child raising responsibility; (c) that children are a liability for female employees; and (d) that women can't handle both work and family responsibilities.

When you need information that may be sensitive, elicit it sensitively. For example, when interviewing an older applicant, don't ask, "Why did you decide to go into this field at your age?" Instead, inquire how that person's prior experience will contribute to his work with your company. Likewise, instead of asking a person whether her spouse will be able to find a job in your city, ask what factors will be important in deciding where she will accept a job or what other cities she is considering and why. These questions are likely to provide you with the same information, without running the risk of offending the interviewee.

Certain questions are definitely impermissible, including questions about age; arrests; citizenship; marital or parental status or plans; and race, religion, sex, or national origin. The Americans with Disabilities Act has greatly expanded the protection afforded persons with disabilities, in some cases requiring an employer to make accommodations that will allow the disabled to work. Though discrimination on the basis of sexual preference is not currently outlawed federally, several cities and states, and some schools, prohibit discrimination on this basis.

Unintentional Discrimination

As indicated earlier, we all think of ourselves as free of bias. Unfortunately, few of us are. Think about whether you may be unintentionally looking at candidates in ways that could be prejudicial.

For example, do you sometimes emerge from an interview with a minority candidate thinking the candidate was "articulate" or "well-educated"? Do you ever have similar reactions to white candidates? If the interviewee went to a respectable college (and perhaps graduate school), ask yourself why you should be surprised he would be articulate or well-educated.

Do you view assertiveness as a virtue in white male candidates, but sometimes regard minority or women candidates as "pushy"?

Do you rule out a minority candidate because of a grammatical mistake or a mispronounced word during the interview? Would you do the same with a white candidate?

Do you think about how you have hired a few minorities who "haven't worked out"? Haven't you hired many whites who haven't worked out, too?

Do you make eye contact with most candidates, but not with disabled candidates? Do you fail to shake hands with disabled candidates? refer to them as "handicapped"?

A client recently spoke to me about his diversity efforts, which he described as trying to hire people who were not "between the tackles." How would that language sound to women, who are not only not found between the tackles, but are not on the football field at all?

To avoid illegal or discriminatory questions, make yourself aware of, and reject, certain common misconceptions that produce biases, for example:

- Young people with long hair use drugs.
- People who shake are alcoholics.
- People who dress unconventionally are radicals.
- The physically disabled have a higher rate of absenteeism.
- Women are not motivated to have careers.
- Older workers cannot accept supervision.

- Non-whites are generally less motivated to work than whites.
- Gays and lesbians are preoccupied with sexual interests that will interfere with their job performance.
- Minorities are primarily interested in issues directly affecting their groups.
- Women are not as tough as men.

Ask yourself whether you may be susceptible to these or other biases. If so, beware of falling prey to them. Biases are obstacles to making sound hiring decisions.

Be aware that comments or jokes may easily be misunderstood by an interviewee. Do not give advice "as a friend" that may be taken as discriminatory by a minority interviewee. Below are a few questions or comments that minorities or women have found offensive:

Are you interested in playing for our company's basketball team?

You are an articulate young lady/man.

Were you admitted/financed through a special program for minorities at your school?

Do you think you could be a team player in this environment?

Asking for standard testing scores (even if asked to give the minority candidate "a break")

What does your dad do?

Are you married or single?

Do you plan to have children?

We have not been able to find qualified minority candidates. (Many minorities view "qualified" as a test applied to them, but not to whites—an additional hurdle for them to jump.)

Women don't normally play on our softball team.

Comments about having a daughter, niece, or female neighbor interested in going into this field.

A Hispanic applicant being asked about Mexican beer.

A Chinese applicant being asked about Chinese food.

An older applicant asked how it would feel to be twice as old as other new employees.

An Asian woman being asked if she thought she was aggressive enough.

If a candidate volunteers information that might be considered discriminatory, you needn't say, "Sorry, I can't talk about that." On the other hand, you should probably not dwell on the topic, or veer further into what may be questionable areas. For example, if an interviewee volunteers that he is the first in his family to attend college, you might respond with, "That's great. You must be very proud of that. How do you think that will affect your performance on the job?" That approach would be far preferable to saying, "Oh, really? What sort of work did your parents and grandparents do?"

Though you may be asking a question or making a comment for benign reasons, discrimination is in the eyes of the beholder—the interviewee. The Equal Employment Opportunity Commission, EEOC, presumes that questions asked in a prejob interview were used as a basis for the hiring decision. The burden is on your company to show that they were not. And, in a real sense, whether you prevail ultimately is irrelevant. The harm has been done when a discrimination charge is made against you.

The Interviewee's Perspective

Interviewers are not the only ones guilty of making discriminatory remarks. Interviewees may demonstrate their bias, either toward the interviewer or in offhand remarks about other groups. Just because you have a shared background with the interviewer does not give you license to make derogatory comments about other groups. Interviewees who reveal their biases during an interview will be ruled out quickly by sensitive interviewers.

As an interviewee, you have every right to object to interview conduct or questions that you regard as discriminatory by the interviewer. Bear in mind, though, that a good deal of discriminatory conduct may be motivated by the genuine curiosity of the interviewer (for example, questions about your family), by ignorance (questions by elderly male interviewers about women's child-rearing plans), by a desire to establish rapport (a question of a black male about a black male professional athlete), or even by a desire to help the interviewee (an interviewer who questions a minority student about his SAT scores thinking that those scores might compensate for a less-than-desirable academic performance).

Benign motivation (or ignorance) does not excuse discriminatory questions. But interviewees should consider whether every question that may be discriminatory is worth reacting to. The greatest danger I see for interviewees who are constantly on the lookout for discriminatory behavior is that it may color their whole approach to the interview process, causing them to take an overly defensive (or aggressive) posture that adversely affects their interview performance. My advice to interviewees is to recognize discriminatory questions when they strike you, but not to search for them.

FOURTEEN

CHECKING REFERENCES

Used properly, reference checks allow you to compensate for the shortcomings of the interview process. You will be able to get the advice of somebody who has experienced firsthand over a period of time what you have been trying to divine indirectly in a brief interview.

Unfortunately, though, interviewers and interviewees often fail to take full advantage of reference checks. References are checked cursorily, if at all, and only so that if anyone asks, you can say, "Yeah, I checked references."

Many reference checkers ask about the person's (or company's) credentials only apologetically, or use a manner and tone of voice that conveys this message: "For God's sake, *please* don't tell me anything bad about this person (or company). We (I) want to make him (accept) an offer." (Several companies have told me that they have never *once* turned down a candidate because of an adverse reference.) If you approach the reference check in that way, you might just as well save the money you'd spend on the phone call.

But you *can* learn something from a reference check, if you set out to do so and think about how to approach it. A reference check is an interview, and all of the principles that apply to getting good information in an interview apply as well to reference checks. That includes, importantly, establishing rapport with the person providing the reference. Since almost all reference checks are conducted by phone, establishing rapport is not so easy. How can you go about doing it?

First of all, when you check a reference, make sure you allow yourself time to do it right. Don't make a call when you have only two minutes to talk. Similarly, ask the person if they have fifteen minutes to talk about the candidate (or job). If they "only have a minute," ask when they have a little more time, schedule an appointment, and call back.

Second, take a few minutes to get to know the reference. Of course, when possible, it's always best to talk with a reference who you, a friend, or co-worker of yours knows. It's far less likely that a friend, or even an acquaintance, will lie (or shade the truth).

When you call, explain your objective in seeking a reference in the same terms as we described the purpose of the ideal job interview in the introduction—to determine whether there is a good match between the individual and the company. In other words, you are not just looking for flaws. That means honest answers to your questions should benefit both the candidate and the company.

Employers should speak with people who actually worked with the candidate. It's far easier for a reference to sing the praises or gloss over the defects of somebody with whom he has not worked. If the person you're contacting has had no firsthand experience with the candidate, ask him who has—and call that person.

When you do speak to somebody with whom the candidate worked, find out how much contact the person had with the candidate. If you are asking a senior officer about work performed by a relatively junior employee, you may find that the senior officer's contact was extremely limited. In that case, the person to whom you should speak is the person who actually supervised the work.

Candidates who are checking references on a prospective employer (whether inquiring about the company or the specific person for whom you would be working) should apply the same principles as employers. Establish rapport, and make sure you are talking to people with firsthand experience. Try to establish whether the reference may be biased. Was she fired by the employer? Is she working for a competitor?

Once you have established a relationship with the reference, your inquiry should focus on the decision criteria you have established and, particularly, those aspects of your criteria that remain in question after the interview. Ask tough questions, and don't accept vague generalities as answers.

For example, the employer should ask what, specifically, were thought to be Joe's strengths (other than that he was "a really nice guy")? What, specifically, were the criticisms of Joe or his work? How many people had that difficulty with Joe? Don't accept a glib statement that it was "just a personality conflict" with one person. What was Joe told in his last review? How does Joe rank with others in his group? If you knew what you know now about Joe, would you have hired him? While many references, understandably, will try to sugarcoat the information they are giving to you, few will actually lie.

A candidate should ask what working for the employer (or particular supervisor) was like. What aspects of the job or the supervisor would the reference change, if he could? Why did the reference leave the company (if he did)? If asked, what would the reference tell a close friend or family member about the job or supervisor?

Generally, the reference check should be performed by the person for whom the candidate will be working after interviews are completed and before a decision is made. Where you are checking something specific that would be a precondition to any offer (for example, whether a candidate has completed a particular course), you may wish to check the reference after the initial screening interview. And if a candidate is currently employed and his employer is unaware of his job search, you may want to make your hiring decision subject to a satisfactory reference check. In any case, be sure you've been authorized to check references before calling.

FIFTEEN

MAKING THE DECISION

After all you have been through—both as interviewer and as interviewee—it would be nice if you could plug the information you gathered from the interview into a computer, press a button, and wait for the correct decision. But no such luck. Worse, not only can't you get the right answer from a computer, no expert can give it to you either.

Principles of Decision Making

What I can do, however, is suggest ten principles that may help you arrive at a sensible decision.

1. *Know your criteria for hiring, or for choosing a position and apply them, using all information available to you.* All of that preparatory work I suggested in chapters 1 and 2 is necessary not only for conducting a good interview, but also for making a sound deci-

sion. Once you've gathered the information you need, you must match it to your criteria.

Be sure to use *all* information available, not only what you hear in the interview. For example, an interviewee should observe how employees greet and treat one another during the course of an interview day because that may reveal a good deal about the working environment. Similarly, as an interviewer, you may learn quite a lot about a candidate's personal skills from how courteous he is to your secretary or the receptionist, and a good deal about an interviewee's common sense or judgment from what he bills on an expense-reimbursement form or chooses to charge at the hotel where you put him up.

2. *Identify the most important criteria for you.* No candidate or job will have everything. Unless you have established some priority to your criteria, you will have difficulty making your decision. Often this is more of a problem for the interviewee than for the interviewer. Most interviewees have not had many job experiences, which makes it difficult to rank your job criteria.

It's a bit like how I felt when I was buying my first house. I had lived in apartments all my life. Now I was trying to compare a house that had a powder room on the first floor to another that was two blocks closer to the train. Without experience, it's not easy to judge the relative importance of those two criteria.

3. *Evaluate the ease of acquiring (or the difficulty of changing) the characteristic in question.* An interviewee who has not picked up the jargon of the trade yet, but who has all of the required job skills, may pick up that jargon quite quickly. But a candi-

date whose resume has two typographical errors is probably not well suited for a proofreader position.

To return to the analogy of buying a house, it would be far easier to add a powder room than it would be to move the house closer to the train. On the other hand, it may be easier to adjust to a longer walk to the train (or to find a substitute) than it would be to have no powder room. Well, nobody said decision making was easy.

4. *Consider the extent to which the characteristic is lacking.*   For example, if salary is important, does the job you are considering pay only marginally below what you had hoped, or significantly below that goal? If you are looking for a candidate who is articulate, ask if the interviewee is merely marginally below that standard or totally unable to communicate?

5. *Consider the impact of the lack of that characteristic.*   For an employer, to what extent will the deficiency impede the candidate performing the key functions of the job? Are there other ways of compensating for this deficiency, perhaps by shifting certain responsibilities to another employee?

   For the employee, will this deficiency make you miserable on the job, or be only a minor annoyance? Is it a problem you will confront daily, or only once or twice a year?

   Distinguish between a short-term and a long-term problem. A candidate, for example, would be foolish to let a job decision be affected by an unsatisfactory physical office environment if he knew the employer was moving to new and improved offices within six months.

6. *Take into account how strong the other characteristics of the candidate or the other aspects of the job are.*

You may be far more willing to tolerate long hours in a job that pays extremely well or involves interesting work than you would in a position that pays only modestly and does not provide much of a challenge. Similarly, an employer who encounters a candidate with extraordinary technical skills may put up with a few rough edges in the candidate's personality.

7. *Do not lose sight of the standards you are applying.* It is easy for an employer to extend offers to candidates because they are "as good as" or "just about as good as" some other marginal candidate to whom they have already extended an offer. This least common denominator approach inevitably leads to a devaluation and erosion of your standards, resulting eventually in hiring people who are ill-suited for the position.

At the same time, employers should be aware of the natural tendency to become conservative about extending offers. Though passing up a potentially good candidate may be a less expensive mistake than hiring one who turns out not to be qualified, if you always make the safe decision, you're bound to pass up a lot of good people (and a disproportionate number of those passed up are likely to be minorities).

8. *Consider the opinions of others, but consider also the others whose opinions you are considering.* An employer may gather comments from eight or ten different employees who have interviewed the candidate. Some of those people may be extremely hard graders, others may like virtually everyone they see. Some of those people may be inclined to be turned off or overly impressed by a single characteristic of the candidate. (Old Joe, who loves anybody who

went to Harvard. Or Heather, who thinks all football players are brain-dead.) It's extremely important that you be aware of those predilections in putting the opinions of others into the hopper and arriving at your decision.

Likewise, candidates may seek the advice of others in making their decisions. If you do, make sure the values and priorities of the people whose opinions you are seeking comport with your own (or if they do not, take those differences into consideration). Make sure you learn whether the opinions you get are based upon firsthand experience or are two or three people removed. If you are talking to somebody with firsthand experience, make sure his views are not colored by his having been dismissed by or not having been extended an offer by the company. Also, make sure that whatever views you obtain are not out-of-date. Companies, like people, change.

9. *Don't be too soft.* As an interviewer or an interviewee, you are likely to run into situations in which you genuinely like the person on the other side of the table. Great. But don't let that unduly color your decision.

An employer is not doing a favor to a candidate who is not qualified for the position by extending her an offer because she likes her. Conversely, an interviewee may find it hard to turn down an interviewer who he genuinely likes and who has been very solicitous of his needs during the recruitment process. Indeed, interviewees often mistakenly think they are breaking the interviewer's heart by turning him down.

When I was interviewing, I got many letters like the following:

Dear Mr. Kanter:

    I would like to thank you for taking time to interview with me at the University of——— and for your generous invitation for a second interview in Chicago. I am honored that a firm with your distinction and clientele would even be interested in me. Unfortunately, I will be unable to accept your invitation for a visit to Chicago. I assure you that my decision is in no way a reflection of my high respect for you or your firm. In large part, my decision is the result of a number of previous commitments to interview with other firms.

The fellow who wrote this letter thought I'd be devastated by his news. But typically, by the time a candidate's letter arrives it is tough to place just who the heck the person was. Though that may be tough for an interviewee to swallow, it should help you to put things into perspective.

    Where you have formed a particularly strong relationship with an interviewer or interviewee, there's nothing wrong with maintaining contact with that person, as a friend. Just don't let the fact that you like the other person lead you to make a poor job or hiring decision.

10. *Avoid making decisions when the pressure is on.* Some of the worst hiring decisions are made *in extremis.* I have seen many employers make expensive hiring mistakes because they were in such immediate need of somebody to fill a slot that they hired the first person to come along. Plan in advance to avoid those crunches. And, if they occur despite your best efforts, involve some dispassionate people in the decision-making process, people who are not feeling the pressure to hire because the person is not being hired into their area.

    For interviewees, the pressure is often self-imposed. Don't place false pressure on yourself to make a decision. You have enough legitimate pressure, sometimes imposed by employers who set unreasonably short deadlines for you to accept their offer. Often you can negotiate an extension of that deadline, if you have a real need for more time. And, if you are unable to extend the deadline, consider seriously whether you want to work for that employer, anyway. If a company places that sort of pressure on you even before you have come to work, what will it be like after you have arrived?

Finally—decide. Ultimately, there's no substitute for applying sound judgment, and just deciding. Once you have all the information, agonizing over your decision for too long a period will only serve to alienate the other person.

As a hiring partner, almost every hiring season there was at least one candidate who I hoped would turn down our offer. By the time the decision date arrived, this candidate had called repeatedly, visited the firm several additional times, and seemed completely incapable of making a decision. I was convinced we had make an error in extending an offer to the candidate.

The same holds true for interviewees confronted with employers who are incapable of making a decision. The message to the interviewee is that she is dealing either with an indecisive company or one that is not interested in her, or both.

Remember that almost every decision you make is a compromise. Focus on making the best available choice, not a perfect one. Then decide.

Common Mistakes in Decision Making

Even interviewers and interviewees who are (or should be) familiar with the principles of making decisions make certain mistakes over and over again that bear directly on the quality of their decisions. Some of those mistakes also affect their ability to conduct the interview. For example, if an interviewer is overly impressed by somebody who is older (mistake number four, below), he is less likely to conduct the type of probing interview that will give him the detailed information he needs. I'll admit that it is far easier to identify some of these mistakes than to avert them. Nonetheless, being aware of the pitfalls should help you avoid some of them.

Interviewer's Mistakes

Here, then, are ten of the most common mistakes interviewers make in assessing candidates. (Note also that many of these mistakes make it difficult for companies to hire a diverse workforce since they tend to encourage replication of their current employees.)

1. *Mistaking glibness for intelligence, or polish for ability* Some interviewees are able to talk easily and fluently. There's a tendency to mistake this for intelligence. This is particularly true when a candidate's resume has one or two items that most every interviewer asks about; as a result, the candidate develops a ready patter.

    Other candidates come across as extremely polished. They are dynamite interviewees. They have prepared themselves well for the process (perhaps been coached well) and can anticipate and answer expected interview questions. Similarly, they have prepared pertinent questions about your company because they have studied the company ahead of time, or have been coached to ask penetrating questions. In short, they play the interview game very well. Though this type of preparation by a candidate may indicate a characteristic that you value on the job, it does not necessarily mean the interviewee possesses the other skills you may be looking for.

It's crucial that you try to distinguish between good interviewees and strong performers. Your best chance of separating out the champion interviewer from the top performer is by not asking the most common interview questions and by probing areas of the interviewee's experience in depth.

2. *Looking for drinking buddies (or for yourself) in each interviewee*   Too many interviewers make a hiring decision based on whether they would like to go out for a drink with the interviewee after work each night. Though you want to hire somebody who will get along with co-workers and customers, your hiring test should not be whether this person is likely to become your best friend. Remember that somebody who comes across in an interview as less than the all-American boy or girl athlete or TV model may be an extremely valuable employee. In fact, don't you have a few of those around your company?

Most of us tend to equate our own backgrounds with the ideal profile of the candidate. Many authors who write for interviewees advise their readers to make an interviewer "see another him in you." Some interviewees are quite adept at converting common experiences and shared values into job offers.

As an interviewer, I've fallen prey to this myself.

For many years, I used to wonder why I hired only bald scuba divers, until it dawned on me one day why that was happening.

Experienced interviewers know that the best person for the job may be someone who possesses traits that the interviewer does *not* have and who can therefore complement her strengths.

3. *Overreacting to first impressions; assuming that somebody who looks the part can play the part* Some interviewees are slower in getting started or in making an impression than others. Don't condemn an interviewee because of a weak handshake, an ugly tie, or a failure to guffaw at your opening joke. Give each interviewee a chance to prove himself, before you write him off.

We sometimes form a picture of the person we envision in a particular job. When an interviewee fits that picture, you may assume that he has the necessary skills. He may not.

4. *Being overly impressed by somebody who's older, or regarding youth as a permanent condition* When comparing someone entering your business or profession as a second career with other candidates who have just graduated from college or graduate school, make sure you are not overly swayed by the fact that this older person seems more mature and streetwise. Conversely, you may interview somebody who has gone straight through college and now is interviewing for his first job. He may appear a bit young, perhaps a little immature. You should not be overly distressed that this younger person needs maturing. That will come. (If the person is wildly inappropriate and juvenile, of course, that is another story.)

5. *Undervaluing motivation* Look around your company. Chances are that many of the people who have

succeeded have done so largely out of a strong desire to get ahead. They may not have had the greatest raw talent. A strong desire to achieve can overcome many other weaknesses. Similarly, a talented person with little motivation will often fail.

6. *Mistaking a quiet or calm manner for lack of motivation* Too many interviewers mistake excitability for (or equate it with) motivation. Quiet, calm determination may evidence at least as much motivation as a hyper, type-A personality.

7. *Overvaluing academic performance* Many of the characteristics interviewers look for in an interviewee are fuzzy, difficult to get a hold of. How do you identify a team player? or somebody who is reliable? So when the interviewer sees a grade point average or a class rank, he may be tempted to say, "Aha, at last, something solid and objective to base my decision on." This search for objectivity often leads interviewers to place too much emphasis on academic performance. Decisions get based on minute differences in overall grade point averages, sometimes a difference of a single grade in one course over an entire college or graduate school career (and without even considering which courses a student excelled in). That's simply a cop-out for thinking about your decision.

Having seen many advertisements listing a top academic record as a prerequisite, I was delighted to see this classified ad in the *Wisconsin Bar Journal*, "Small firm in promising Northwestern Wisconsin location wishes another member. Unquestionable character, discretion, integrity, loyalty, and reasonable amount of intelligence required. Send resume to Box 015, Wisconsin State Bar Center." That ad has the importance of intelligence sized up just about right.

8. *Thinking Harvard and Yale graduates walk on water*   This might be phrased "assuming somebody who looks the part on paper can play the part on the job." Though many graduates of prestigious universities perform extremely well, they all don't walk on water. Indeed, I've seen plenty who drown in shallow water. Many of them are overly impressed with themselves, or unwilling to do the nitty-gritty work involved in most any job.

   This tendency to overestimate the importance of a degree from a prestigious university is often a problem both for graduates of that university and for people who did not graduate from those kinds of universities, but wish they had. For the latter, hiring people from those schools may be a way of confirming to the interviewer that he is just as good as the person he is hiring.

9. *Overvaluing an experience that allows somebody to talk your language and may give the person a short head start in your business*   For example, an interviewee who has a relative in your business may be able to talk a good game, using terminology other interviewees will not be familiar with. Though this familiarity may give the interviewee a short head start on the job, it is an advantage that will not likely be important in the long run.

10. *Overlooking certain missing characteristics or skills necessary to the job because a person is particularly strong in one characteristic*   This is often called the "halo effect." An interviewer may be overwhelmed by a candidate's academic performance and fail to see that the interviewee lacks the interpersonal skills

needed to succeed. Or another interviewer may be dazzled by the interviewee's athletic prowess and overlook necessary job skills.

Lesson for Interviewees: Interviewee's Mistakes

You can safely assume that most of the people who interview you will be prone to making the above mistakes. Recognizing that will enable you to help them avoid them. For example, assume you are the low-key person described in Interviewer's Mistakes number six, above. At an appropriate point in the interview, you may want to say, "You know, I sometimes surprise people. I come across as rather calm and low-key, but I'm actually very tenacious when I set my mind to something." Of course, you should be prepared to give an example of that tenacity.

Let's turn now to the five most common mistakes interviewees make in selecting an employer (because interviewees are twice as smart as interviewers, they make only half as many mistakes):

1. *Being overly impressed by bigness or prestige* As an interviewee, you may be wowed by the size or prestige of the company, and that may blind you to taking into account other considerations. Your reaction may not only lead you to a poor job decision, it may also cause you to listen and probe less critically during the interview.

   Being overly impressed by bigness or prestige is a little like the halo effect in interviewers. This is especially a problem in a campus interview, where students sometimes feel the need to impress their classmates by accepting jobs from a big or prestigious employer.

2. *Undervaluing lifestyles considerations* Sure, it's important to find stimulating, interesting work, excellent
training, and a stable economic situation. But remember that you will be spending a very significant part
of your waking hours on your job. The type of people
you work with, the physical environment, the flexibility to do other things you may be interested in, and
to have a life outside of work are extremely important.

An interviewer friend of mine told me he once
asked an interviewee, "What kind of place would make
you feel happy to come to work in the morning?"
She gave him a deadpan look, and replied, "In the
late–twentieth century, one does not take account of
happiness—does one?" Don't believe that.

3. *Spending your life maximizing your options* Making
a job decision can be extremely scary. Many interviewees tend to look for and select a position they feel
will maximize their future options. Up to a point,
that's fine. Too often, however, this desire to maximize one's options gets in the way of making decisions about what is important to you.

For example, I have seen too many partners in
law firms who have gone to law school because they
couldn't think what else to do, and law provided many
options. They chose the most prestigious law school
they could get into because that would maximize their
options upon graduation. After the second year of
law school, they chose to work for a large law firm
because that would expand their options the next
year. Upon graduation, they accepted a job in the
biggest city with the largest and most prestigious firm
who would hire them, chose to practice in several
different areas of law, and stayed around for eight
years to make partner—all in the name of maximizing
their options. Now they're fifty and perceive that they

have no options except to stay where they are (if they can). Don't regard maximizing your options as a career.

4. *Looking for yourself in the interviewer; being overly impressed with an interviewer* Interviewees also tend to gauge whether they would fit into a company by whether they see themselves in the interviewer. Doing this assumes that everyone at the company is the same, or that you can work only with people who are just like you. A smart interviewee values diversity as much as a smart interviewer.

And just because an interviewer impresses you does not mean the employer is a good choice for you. After all, any company should have at least one impressive person they can put forward. Remember that the person who interviews you may have little or no contact with you if you were to join the company.

Of course, you can go to the other extreme, as well. Robert Half International, an executive and professional recruiting company in the financial industry, conducted a survey in which vice-presidents and personnel directors of one hundred large corporations were asked to describe their most unusual experience interviewing prospective employees. One person reported a candidate who asked to see the interviewer's resume to see if the personnel executive was qualified to judge him as the candidate.

5. *Failure to identify what you are looking for in a company* Unless you have prepared adequately for the interview process, you will waste a lot of time. In addition, you may deny other potential candidates a fair opportunity to interview with the company. And, if you do not identify what you are looking for during the entire interview process, you may wind up in a job for which you are ill-suited.

Time of Day

One final caution in making decisions. Both the interviewer and the interviewee should recognize that the time of day you see someone will affect your impressions of that person, and therefore your decision. Late in the afternoon, both the interviewee and the interviewer are likely to be tired, and that fatigue is likely to affect both people's performances, as well as their ability to listen. Both parties should recognize this time-of-day phenomenon, expend extra effort to try to overcome it, and factor it into their decision-making process.

SIXTEEN

THE OFFER, FOLLOW-UP, AND CLOSING

Recruiting rarely ends with the interview. When is the last time you ended an interview by saying, "I'd like to offer you the position," and had the interviewee reply, "Great, when do I start?" Usually you have to follow up with an interviewee in order to close the deal.

The Offer

Even employers who have given considerable thought to the recruitment process often treat making an offer as a perfunctory formality. They never think much about it, nor do they recognize its potential as a selling tool.

Reasonable employers may differ as to whether an offer should be extended on the same day an interviewee visits the company. In part, the answer may depend upon the length of your recruitment process. If that process involves several visits to the company and extensive interviews, you may be able to make the decision on the day of the candidate's last visit.

I prefer not to make an offer the day a candidate visits the company. For one thing, it prevents an orderly and thorough consideration of candidates. It is difficult, if not impossible, to collect comments from everybody the interviewee has seen, to evaluate those comments and to compare the interviewee with other candidates you may have seen. (One definite advantage of extending an offer when the candidate is in the office, though, is that you can do it in person.)

Some employers feel that making an offer on the day a candidate visits is a powerful selling tool. It shows a decisive company, they argue, and one clearly interested in the candidate. That may be so, but it does not show a deliberate company, or one that takes the offer process seriously. Many candidates, even top candidates, like to feel that a company has gone through a thorough evaluation process before extending them an offer. These candidates regard an offer received at the time they visit as a "cheap" offer.

Whether you extend the offer in person or by telephone, keep three principles in mind. First, you want to make the offer with enthusiasm, rather than conveying the impression that the offer is being extended by virtue of a seven-to-six vote in favor of the candidate. Part of what sells a candidate is a sense that the company really wants him. In extending the offer, you may want to congratulate the candidate because you want her to feel that receiving the offer is an accomplishment.

Second, make the offer more personal by mentioning something favorable you recall about your interaction with the person. Or, alternatively, refer to something about the person that others at your company commented upon positively.

Third, use the offer conversation to gather information

that may be helpful in hiring the person. Make sure you know where, when, and how the person can be reached, and gather whatever information you can regarding the status of her decision-making process, her concerns, your principal competition, and the likely timing of her decision. This information will be useful in the follow-up process.

Even when you are rejecting a candidate, you should sell your company. (Remember that the candidate you reject may later become a customer of the company or may be a good friend of another candidate you are trying to hire.) Be as sensitive and helpful as you can in the course of rejecting a candidate. Where appropriate, suggest other avenues the candidate may wish to pursue.

Follow-up

Especially when you are engaged in a recruitment effort at a university, follow-up is critical. Your objective should be to make the candidate feel loved, but not bothered. Exercise central control over the type and frequency of these contacts through whoever is in charge of your recruitment efforts. You may wish to escalate the level of the person contacting the interviewee, i.e., use a more senior officer, as decision time approaches.

Pay attention to the timing of your follow-up. Frequent contacts early in an interview season, at a time when the candidate is not apt to be making a decision, are not likely to be productive and may well annoy the candidate. On the other hand, a contact around decision-making time may make the difference between attracting a candidate or not.

Many candidates are hard to reach on the phone so letters may be a more efficient means of follow-up with a candidate, and certainly will be easier. An occasional phone call in the evening, however, is effective. Where convenient, plan a lunch or dinner or a visit to the company (either for local candidates or for out-of-town candidates when they are in town visiting other companies).

There's no rule as to who should be doing the follow-up contact. Both senior and junior people may be effective, depending upon the circumstances. A person (or persons) who established good rapport with the candidate, either on campus or in the company, should be assigned to follow up with each candidate who is extended an offer. Where out-of-town candidates are involved, a contact by a company employee who happens to have business in the town in which the candidate is located can be very effective, even if that employee has had no prior contact with the candidate. Even when a candidate is in your area, you may ask an employee who you would have liked to see the candidate (but who was not available) to contact the candidate. Besides being flattering to the candidate, contact by somebody the candidate has not met before demonstrates that people at the company talk to one another. That may be especially effective in overcoming concerns about the large size of a company.

Closing

Closing is the process of helping (not pushing) candidates to make decisions that are good for them. Making a decision is difficult for candidates, both because the decision is often perceived to be an important, lifetime commitment, and because the job-seeking process fosters indecision, and encourages candidates to maximize their options.

Most decisions are compromises—choosing the best available, not the perfect choice. Your job in closing is to show the candidate why your company is the best available decision for her. Often, that decision will be made on intangibles such as the "atmosphere" at the company (the cliché for salespersons is "sell on the tangible, close on the intangible").

Of course, the timing of closing will depend on factors such as what interviews the candidate may have left. But too many employers resist trying to close because they fear being rejected. As long as the offer is outstanding, they "still have a chance." But trying for an early close may assist you in several ways: (a) you will find out where you stand; (b) you may gain more information that is useful in closing later; (c) you may succeed in closing; and (d) if you are rejected, you will be able to focus your attention on other real prospects. So don't be afraid to ask a candidate to accept an offer, or to explain what his hesitations in accepting are.

Throughout the follow-up and closing process, you should use information you have gathered during your interviews. By focusing on a candidate's particular concerns and interests, you will show your genuine interest in him and be able to direct your follow-up and closing efforts to what really matters.

Interviewee's Perspective

Interviewees may have occasion to follow up, as well. You may wish to send a personal letter to an interviewer, thanking her for the time she spent with you. One caution, though. Do not follow up merely to show off your word processing prowess. Employers are not impressed by form letters sent to each person you interviewed with during a day at the company. And you may rest assured that your letters will be compared by those who receive them. One letter is quite sufficient; more than sufficient if you have nothing special to say. Save postage—and trees.

Indeed, in the wrong hands, a word-processing system can be a dangerous weapon. Consider this letter received by a prominent law firm:

Dear: _____

I am currently a third-year student at _____ School of Law. Because of the number of students participating in the on-campus interviews this year, I was unable to interview with you during your recent visit to _____. Because I am interested in working for 60606, I am writing to request an interview.

I have enclosed a copy of my resume. As you can see, I have a strong academic background and have done work for several types of law firms.

Again I am very excited at the prospect of meeting with you to discuss employment possibilities at 60606.

Any consideration given this request will be appreciated. I look forward to hearing from you.

Very truly yours,

The poor student had substituted the firm's zip code for the firm name. Or, from the other side of the table, consider the tale I was told by a friend who sent "personalized" rejection letters to a group of interviewees only to find, after the letters were mailed, that the word processor ID below his signature said "form rejection letter no. 2."

Should you find that you need additional information to make your job decision, you should not hesitate to ask for it. And if you were not able to see a sufficient number of people at the company, or if a key player was not available when you visited, a request to spend more time at the company may be perfectly appropriate. Do all of this in moderation, though. Make one request for additional information, not six separate requests for six different items from six different people. Visit the company one more time, not three. The impression you create between the time an offer is extended to you and the time you accept it will stick with you once you arrive at the company.

If you have not received a decision from the company within the time they told you you would, or especially if you need to hear earlier because of a deadline imposed by another job offer, don't hesitate to call the company. A company may be able to decide more quickly than it otherwise would if it knows that you need to hear. It would be foolish for you to rule out an employer you are truly interested in without warning them that you need a decision.

To the extent that you are the recipient of follow-up from an employer, be enthusiastic and be honest. Show appreciation for receiving an offer, even if you expect to reject it. Remember that you may be dealing with people at the company as colleagues in your industry or as customers or clients, or you may be seeking a position with the company later in your career.

During the follow-up, be honest with the employer as to the status of your decision-making process. When you have eliminated an employer, reject its offer even if you have not decided which offer you will accept. Do that in fairness to the employer and to other candidates for the position. After all, you would want other candidates for positions you may be interested in to do that for you.

Try not to resent being "bothered" by follow-up from the employer. Regard calls and letters as signs the company is truly interested in you. If you really do feel harassed by follow-up, try tactfully to let your prospective employer know, either by indicating that you will not be in a position to make a decision for a period of time and will call them as soon as you know, or by saying that you are flattered by all of the attention, but you now think you have all of the information you will need about the company to make a decision.

Finally, when you accept an offer, do it with enthusiasm. Remember, accepting an offer may be the end of the recruitment process, but it is the beginning of your job with the company. Start that job out on the right foot.

SEVENTEEN

BEYOND THE INTERVIEW GAME

Somebody once defined an interviewer as "an unqualified observer who makes extensive inferences based on limited data obtained in an artificial setting." That same person might define an interviewee as "a terrified participant who provides rehearsed answers based on uninformed guesses as to what interviewers might be looking for." I hope this book alters those definitions for you—on both sides of the table. Only informed interviewers and interviewees who understand both the possibilities and limitations of the interview process will get beyond the interview game.

Throughout this book we have seen what causes the interview to become a game—inadequate preparation, poor questions and answers, a one-side-of-the-table-only perspective, ineffective communication, and more. Too often, these mistakes transform interviewing from the exciting adventure it should be into an empty ritual.

Each step of the interview process directly affects other steps. When you fail to identify what you are looking for, you are unable to ask the right questions. Failure to ask the right questions, to answer questions properly, and to sell yourself and handle obstacles effectively all lead to poor information. Poor information leads to bad decision-making. And any of these failures may lead to claims of discrimination. Thus a lapse into the interview game at any stage may contaminate the entire process.

To avoid the interview game, you must appreciate not only the possibilities of an interview, but also its limitations. Interviewing is an imperfect process. Though both interviewers and interviewees crave certainty and objectivity, alas, it cannot be. These are *people* you are hiring, not objects. A modicum of subjectivity is unavoidable, and desirable.

But it is precisely because an interview involves people, not objects, that interviewing can prove so fascinating. And so much fun. When it's done right, each interview becomes energizing and distinctive. I recall, even cherish, many of my interview experiences. And some of those I interviewed have become my lifelong friends.

Earlier, I suggested that interviewers should be curious. So should interviewees. The word "curious" comes from a Latin word meaning "to care." If you care about the people you are speaking to, the questions you ask and the answers you receive, if you care enough to take the time to understand the interview from both sides of the table, you will be well on your way to getting beyond the interview game.

Interviewing has long-term impact. People recall good and bad interview experiences years, even decades, after they occur. The content of those interviews may fade in memory, but the impressions linger on. People sitting across the interview table from one another become co-workers, competitors, clients, suppliers, customers, colleagues, and friends. Taking a short-term view of this long-term effect defies common sense, and encourages gamesmanship.

The cornerstone of getting beyond the interview game

is honesty. An interviewer or interviewee may gain a short-term advantage by being less than candid. But lack of candor leads in the long run to poor hiring decisions, poor job selection, personal unhappiness, excessive turnover, and enormous costs, both financial and human.

Not only does honesty lead to good decisions, it also sells—for both sides of the table. Even in a competitive market, candor works because it is seen so rarely in an interview setting. Candor is the secret weapon—both for getting and giving the information you need and for selling your company or yourself effectively.

The ideal interview world we conjured in the introduction need not remain a fairy tale. You can create that world in your own interviews and, in so doing, push both sides of the table beyond the interview game.

Appendix

PRINCIPAL FEDERAL STATUTES
BEARING ON NON-DISCRIMINATION
IN EMPLOYMENT

Civil Rights Act of 1981	42 USC 1981–88
Age Discrimination in Employment Act of 1967	29 USC 621–34
Veterans' Reemployment Rights	38 USC 4301–07
Glass Ceiling Act of 1991	Pub. L. 102–166, Title II, Nov. 21, 1991, 105 Stat. 1081 (Title 42 Sec. 2000e note)
Americans with Disabilities Act of 1990	42 USC 12101–213
Title VII of Civil Rights Act of 1964	42 USC 2000e et seq.
Rehabilitation Act	29 USC 701–797B
Pregnancy Discrimination Act	42 USC 2000e(k)

Bibliography

Here are a few of the more worthwhile books on interviewing, some from each side of the table:

Allen, Jeffrey. *How to Turn an Interview Into a Job.* New York: Simon and Schuster, 1983.

Caple, John. *The Ultimate Interview.* New York: Doubleday, 1991.

Catalyst staff. *When Can You Start? The Complete Job-Search Guide for Women of All Ages.* New York: Macmillan Publishing Co., Inc., 1981.

Drake, John D. *The Effective Interviewer: A Guide for Managers.* New York: American Management Association, 1989.

Goodale, James. *The Fine Art of Interviewing.* Englewood Cliffs, New Jersey: Prentice-Hall, 1982.

Kennedy, Jim. *Getting Behind the Resume: Interviewing Today's Candidates.* Paramus, New Jersey: Prentice-Hall Information Services, 1987.

Krannich, Caryl Rae and Ronald L. *Interview for Success: A Practical Guide to Increasing Job Interviews, Offers and Salaries,* 3d ed. Woodbridge, Virginia: Impact Publications, 1990.

Medley, H. Anthony. *Sweaty Palms: The Neglected Art of Being Interviewed*, rev. ed. Berkeley: Ten Speed Press, 1992.

Merman, Stephen and John McLaughlin. *Out Interviewing the Interviewer: The Job Winner's Script for Success*. Englewood Cliffs, New Jersey: Prentice-Hall, 1983.

Pettus, Theodore T. *One on One: Win the Interview, Win the Job*. New York: Random House, 1981.

Ryan, Joseph. *Stating Your Case: How to Interview for a Job as a Lawyer*. St. Paul, Minnesota: West Publishing Company, 1982.

Ryckman, W. G. *How to Pass the Employment Interview (with flying colors)*. Homewood, Illinois: Dow Jones-Irwin, 1982.

Smart, Bradford D., *The Smart Interviewer: Tools and Techniques for Hiring the Best*. New York: John Wiley & Sons, 1989.

Uris, Auren. *88 Mistakes Interviewers Make . . . And How to Avoid Them*. New York: American Management Association, 1988.

Vlk, Suzee. *Interviews That Get Results: Mastering the Job-Getting Strategies That Make the Difference*. New York: Monarch Press, 1984.

INDEX

ABOUT THE AUTHOR

ARNOLD KANTER serves as a consultant to law firms and investment banks on hiring and related issues. He has taught interview training widely around the country. Prior to starting his consulting practice, Kanter was a partner in a large national law firm, Sonnenschein Nath and Rosenthal. He is the author of seven other books, including *Kanter on Hiring*. He graduated from Brandeis University and holds a J.D. degree from Northwestern University School of Law and an LL.M. from The London School of Economics.